Paul Powell

The Fighting Dragon: How to Defeat the Yugoslav Attack

MONGOOSE
Press

BOSTON

Publisher: Mongoose Press
1005 Boylston Street, Suite 324
Newton Highlands, MA 02461
info@mongoosepress.com
www.MongoosePress.com

ISBN: 978-1-936277-74-2
Library of Congress Control Number: 2016911222

Distributed to the trade by National Book Network
custserv@nbnbooks.com, 800-462-6420
For all other sales inquiries please contact the Publisher.

Layout: Stanislav Makarov
Editor: Jorge Amador
Cover Design: Alexander Krivenda
Printed in the United States of America

First English edition
0 9 8 7 6 5 4 3 2 1

Contents

Book 2: Quizzes

Preface

My first chess book, *Chess Patzer to Master – How an Everyday Joe Does It,* is a message of hope for the average chessplayer. Improving at chess is not a straightforward process whereby immersing yourself in the deeply annotated games of the world's greatest players will provide you wisdom by osmosis. On the contrary, you need to learn many other skills, from trusting your instincts and mastering your emotions to channeling your fear of failure and taming an overambitious desire to win at all costs. It is also essential to master basic endgames, change the way you think about life, and – yes – some carefully crafted osmosis is always good!

Pattern Recognition

Extending the ideas presented in *Chess Patzer to Master,* it is my hope that *The Fighting Dragon* will be the first in a series of books that presents inspiration and pattern recognition instead of memorization as a critical element of your opening studies. Yes, in *Chess Patzer to Master* I do recommend studying endgames, because opening theories come and go like the seasons. Still, let me be very clear: to avoid the study of openings entirely would be a mistake. What I don't agree with is for a 1600-rated player to purchase a $25 book with 350 pages of advice on how to play one specific cutting-edge opening, or (worse yet) one specific line in an opening. Inevitably, the novice player lacks the ability to learn all the lines covered in the book, and even if he or she has an exceptional memory and commits these intricate lines to memory, they will never face a player skilled enough to play any variation twenty-three moves deep. Worse yet, experienced players know that some young upstarts can commit these texts to memory, so they avoid these main lines like a zombie virus. What typically happens, then, is that the novice player who has invested all this time learning these book lines will face an amateur who deviates at random from main-line theory and the novice has no idea how to punish the amateur.

Enlightenment

This is where this book comes to the rescue. Do this exercise: close your eyes and lightly press your fingertips on your eyelids. See those flashing, swirling lights? You have now reached enlightenment and are ready for the next phase of learning.

OK, not really. You can't truly see "anything" inside your eyes. What you are experiencing is the pressure on the retinal artery cutting off the blood supply to the retina. Deprived of oxygen, the photoreceptors start firing, giving you the impression that you are seeing swirling colors or flashing lights.

There are those of a mystical bent who will say this little exercise assists the mind in becoming ready for enlightenment. Those of a scientific bent might say, "Oxygen deprivation to the photoreceptors proves that there is nothing magical taking place." Yet the careful observer should note that the position neither of the mystical nor of the scientific mind has any influence on the outcome. When you press against your closed eyelids, you do see lights, regardless of which story you believe. And now I will impart to you the same miracle for chess: follow the process and you'll improve your game. Call it enlightenment and believe in the process, or not. It doesn't matter if you believe in the following process; follow it, and it will work for you. Before we get to the process, though, I would like to share my inspiration for this method.

ZOOM 001

One of my favorite chess books is the Danish grandmaster Bent Larsen's *ZOOM 001: Zero Hour for Operative Opening Models.* Larsen's model for the book is pattern recognition. Larsen tried to expand this pattern recognition into a complete system that could be played for Black or White and in all phases of the game. That is a bit ambitious for my taste, so we'll key in on just the concept of pattern recognition as a timeless skill.

Preface

As a master, I loved *ZOOM 001,* and as a young patzer, I was deeply indebted to GM William Lombardy's *Modern Chess Opening Traps,* a simple book filled with snares and pitfalls that I used to cut my tactical teeth as a youngster. Now, all these years later, I pressed my fingers on my eyes and saw the light: by connecting the Master and the Patzer, I saw the solution to learning sharp openings such as the Dragon: connect the pattern ideas with quick tactical wins.

The problem that the novice faces when setting out to plumb the depths of opening knowledge is that it never provides the desired result. As we've seen, top-level GMs avoid the deep analysis, while amateurs lack the skills to deviate in a logical way – instead, they wander off into some obscure footnote in the book that may not be well documented. Neither result is a desirable outcome for the booked-up player.

Now that you know about both the enlightenment myth and *ZOOM 001,* this is how we are going to apply it.

Book 1: Ideas and Patterns

Introduction

Welcome to *The Fighting Dragon,* where you will achieve chess enlightenment. OK, full disclosure: you might not reach enlightenment by reading this book and you might not learn the wisdom of the ages by osmosis. But that's really all right, because enlightenment is highly overrated: it's the journey that matters. Our journey starts with this book, by reviewing games where Black won in a short number of moves. These types of games are known as miniature games and by their very nature they are contests where a major mistake was made. Therefore, we don't look to these games for deep theory. What we can learn from these games are tactical themes, which you can use to find patterns in your own games.

Once you complete this book, you'll be ready for the next step in the journey, which requires that you take the knowledge and insight you've gained to develop a plan that's tailored for you. I'll have more to say about this soon.

How to Enter the Multiverse

Now that you have received enlightenment, I would like to share another gift with you; you simply have to be willing to take an existential leap of faith with me. The concept comes from String Theory in physics, and it is called a "multiverse," or parallel universes. Before you have thoughts of putting this book down, you should know that many well-known theoretical physicists believe in multiverses, including Stephen Hawking, Brian Greene, and Max Tegmark. So let's take this a step deeper and consider M-theory, which has its own view of a multiverse squeezed into one of its 10 or 11 space-time dimensions. Or, if you prefer, we can take the more generic view where they exist in many universes parallel to us, and are just like us but are doing something different.

As crazy and as mind-boggling as it sounds, this is actually mainstream science. As the story goes, somewhere in one of these parallel universes someone is doing exactly what you are doing right now, except that instead of reading this next line, they stop and go get a cup of coffee. In another universe, they are reading the book but using their left hand to turn the pages instead of their right. In still another, they are reading right to left instead of left to right. Stripping away all the high-end science, what this means to us in our personal day-to-day life is that at any given moment we only have one choice. Maybe I can't give you enlightenment and I can't transport you to a multiverse, or maybe I can.

Let's be totally honest: most of us get into a life rut. We follow the "lather, wash, rinse, repeat" sequence with very little variation. You might have a closet with 28 shirts and 12 pairs of pants, but most folks stuck in the rut will wear three pairs of pants over and over and maybe cycle in and out nine different shirts. They'll eat the same menu items and use the same catchphrases. It's just human nature.

Our behaviors, thoughts, and patterns in our everyday life will filter down to how we approach our chess life: what openings we play, what type of positions we favor, and our comfort zones. We become so hidebound in protecting our boundaries that we'll go into a losing chess line or make a bad life decision because the space is comfortable. Yet in another universe, we are bold, we are heroes – and we are winners. Let's take a deeper look at the rut and at how we can achieve our own enlightenment and multiverse experience.

The Rut

Once you pass the beginner stage, it's easy to fall into an opening repertoire rut. You learn an opening line and achieve some level of success while at the same time getting increasingly comfortable with the positions that come out of that opening. The comfort turns into complacency and you stop exploring, stop taking chances, and settle for what you know. In metaphysical terms, this is the very essence of being trapped into a "single chess universe," limiting your chess horizons. If you have a difficult time accepting these traits in yourself, let us segue to your local chess club. Do you know someone who's been playing for over 20 years and always trotting out the same old lines? What about the club member who's rated 1500 and always plays the Blackmar-Diemer Gambit as White? Or the 1942-rated player who's well known for the Winawer Variation of the French Defense but nothing else? Yes, both are trapped in their own repertoire and most likely you are, too – or will become so, sooner or later.

Let us consider the Dragon player who is stuck in a rut. He revels in showing you his favorite game from 2002 where he crushed a master in the main-line Dragon. Great result, but sadly for him he's been playing the exact same line for over a decade in the hopes that another strong player will fall down the same rabbit hole. He plays on autopilot, and if White plays moves that reach the following position regardless of the move order, Black won't even start to think until this main-line Dragon position is reached.

1.e4 c5 2.♘f3 d6 3.d4 cxd4 4.♘xd4 ♘f6 5.♘c3 g6 6.♗e3 ♗g7 7.f3 0-0 8.♕d2 ♘c6 9.♗c4 ♗d7 10.0-0-0 ♖c8:

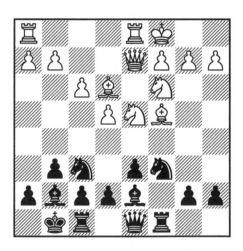

Sadly, we tell him the story of one of these parallel universes where someone is sitting down to play chess who looks just like him and the only difference at this exact moment in time is that after

1.e4 c5, they are putting on their proverbial thinking cap, whereas our friend trapped in our universe won't wake up for another nine moves. Image we tell our friend, "Here is a golden ticket to a parallel universe. Would you like to go explore?" and he simply replies, "No, this is what I always do." I mean, really? Who wouldn't jump at the chance to explore a new universe, assuming there is no life-threatening risk like being sucked into a black hole! Of course you'd say yes! At least I hope you would. Learn to live, let go, and experience new things.

Remember that nobody in life will ever take care of you as well as you take care of yourself. You've got to get in there and do the work. But let me share some ideas on what that work involves:

1. Do not take any single idea from this book and make it your new main line. Instead, take at least three or four main ideas and mix your play up each time you play the Dragon.

2. After each game, make notes and try to find ways to improve your play; do this for each idea that you've chosen to follow more deeply.

3. Try to play at least five or six games with each idea; they do not have to be full-blown tournament games. However, do try to at least play 20- or 30-minute games; using 5-minute chess to explore deep opening ideas is always a bad plan.

4. After you start to develop a feel for the new ideas, trim your exploration down to two or three ideas that you will investigate in greater depth, and repeat. At no time, though, should you ever revert to playing one "main line."

5. Take on the mindset that you are in this to improve your play over time and not to win a quick game by learning a trap or two. Once you feel very comfortable in several Dragon lines, you'll have more than one tool in your toolbox that you can unleash to fit your opponent or your mood.

A New Beginning

From this moment forward, we are going to start thinking sooner; we will no longer follow blindly down the main-line Dragon. If White deviates from the move order, we will learn what new patterns and ideas we might explore. If he tries to steer steady as a rock toward the main line, we'll mix up our moves and try new ideas. We'll take a leap of faith and let go of what is comfortable, and by trying new ideas and reaching new positions and patterns, we will expand our overall ability. Our parallel universes will be filled with ideas like 9...♘d7, 9...♘xd4, 9...♕a5, and others.

Do you think I'm being melodramatic? Imagine for a moment that your entire chess life is filled with playing positions that fork out from 9...♗d7!?. An entire "life," an entire "universe of your experience," is limited by your failure to explore equal (or nearly equal) ideas.

So let's create a goal for this new experience:

I will explore new ideas and open my mind to new patterns. I will learn new patterns and become a stronger player.

Failure is not measured by wins and losses; failure is continuing to play without learning.

I will not be afraid to play these ideas in blitz, bullet, or even regular tournament games. I will not worry about winning or losing rating points. I will only concern myself with learning from each game that I play. I will not play with a fear of losing. I will embrace the spirit of a warrior.

As you explore and learn, bear in mind what Sun Tzu wrote in *The Art of War*: "Do not repeat the tactics which have gained you one victory, but let your methods be regulated by the infinite variety of circumstances."

Let's clear our minds and begin our journey.

9.♗c4 ♘d7

Game 1

MacDonald, Jonathan – Zube, M. [B77]
Nuremberg 1989

1.e4 c5 2.♘f3 d6 3.d4 cxd4 4.♘xd4 ♘f6 5.♘c3 g6 6.♗e3 ♗g7 7.f3 ♘c6 8.♕d2 0-0 9.♗c4 ♘d7

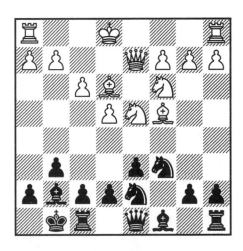

Black retreats his knight to d7. What ideas do you see? Take a minute before reading further, and think about Black's plans and options. One benefit to ...♘d7 is that the g7-bishop and the c6-knight apply combined pressure on the d4 square. That pressure on d4 slows White down from playing an early ♗h6, unless he is willing to exchange at c6 first, lest the d4-knight be left hanging. If White exchanges on c6, it opens the b-file for us and our rook goes to b8, putting pressure on White's queenside. Another idea is that the knight at d7 can travel to e5, attacking c4, just like the c6-knight can go to e5 and c4. This tandem-knights approach means that if we get to c4 and White chops the knight off with his light-squared bishop, we still have another knight in the pipeline waiting to control c4. Also note that the d7-knight can travel to b6, pressuring c4 from there, too. This "tandem knights" idea will give White a lot to worry about unless he is familiar with these positions.

10.0-0-0 ♞b6 11.♗b3 ♞a5

White trots out natural developing Yugoslav moves, which plays into Black's plan of maneuvering the knights to harass the light- and dark-squared bishops.

12.♗h6

If White is trying to avoid the exchange of the dark-squared bishop that was threatened by ...♞bc4, this is not the way to go about it.

12...♞bc4 13.♛g5 e5 14.♞db5 ♗f6

If White saw this punch coming, he missed the next one.

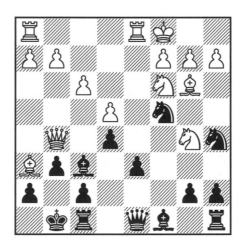

15.♛g3 ♗h4

Black traps the queen and knocks White out with a one-two to the ribs.

16.♗xf8 ♗xg3 17.♗xd6 ♗f4+ 18.♔b1 ♞d2+ 19.♔a1 a6 20. ♗c7 ♞axb3+ 21.cxb3 ♞xb3+ 22.axb3 axb5+ 0-1

Now let's look at another game with ...♘f6-d7 where White tries a different method of handling this odd-looking knight move.

Game 2

Blanco Sánchez, José Fernando – Gavin Roche, Enrique [B77]
Hermano Adolfo Open, Zaragoza (Spain) 1991

1.e4 c5 2.♘f3 d6 3.d4 cxd4 4.♘xd4 ♘f6 5.♘c3 g6 6.♗e3 ♗g7 7.♗c4 0-0 8.f3 ♘c6 9.♕d2 ♘d7 10.0-0-0 ♘b6 11.♗b3 ♘a5

A point worth noting is that the move order is not exactly the same in this game as the previous one. In the previous game, White played f2-f3 on move seven, while here he plays 7.♗c4. As a general rule, unless you know exactly how to punish a deviation in the move order (assuming such a punishment exists), do not try to figure it out over the board. You are more likely to find yourself at the bottom of a rabbit hole with no way out. Had Black tried to punish White for not playing 7.f3 with 7...♘g4, he would have found that, after 8.♗b5+, he must play 8...♔f8 with the worse position, as interposing at d7 drops the g4-knight and 8...♘c6 drops an exchange. However, not all transpositions are harmless for White. For example, should he castle before ♗c4, he will provide Black an opportunity to break in the center (covered later), and that opportunity will most likely arise on move 9.

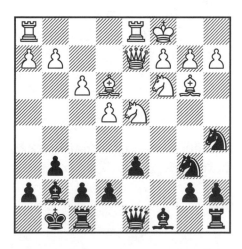

12.♕e2

In the previous game, White launched the bishop into h6 to attack, whereas here White tries to contain the position by anchoring off against the c4 square. Bravo for playing with restraint.

12...♘xb3+ 13.axb3 ♗d7 14.h4 a5

Now, in typical Dragon fashion, both sides race to deliver mate. At this point, neither side has a clear advantage, but I think we can safely assume that Black has had more experience in these positions, as ...♘d7 is his main line.

15.h5 a4 16.bxa4 ♘xa4

It seems logical for White to capture the pawn with 16.bxa4. However, there is something to be said for ignoring the queenside and playing all out on the kingside. With this series of exchanges, White is creating additional targets for Black.

17.hxg6 hxg6 18.g4 ♘xc3 19.bxc3 ♕a5

Now the race is really on. Black's threat is ...♕xc3 and mate with the rook at a1. White can continue the counterattack, but only with extraordinary care.

20.♕h2 f6

A forced move. Tricks like 20...♖fc8 lead to disaster after 21.♕h7+ ♔f8 22.♗h6 ♕a1+ 23.♔d2 ♕xc3+ 24.♔e2 ♗b5+ 25.♘xb5 ♕c4+ 26.♔f2 ♔e8 27.♘xd6+ exd6 28.♕xg7, and Black's attack fizzles.

21.♕h7+ ♔f7 22.♗h6

Chess is a hard game. The very unnatural 22.♖h6! offers better chances than the natural-looking 22.♗h6.

22...♖g8 23.♘f5

White fails at the delicate task of knowing when to defend and when to attack. On 23.♘e2 instead, it's still a game.

23...♕xc3

Now White realizes that mate can't be stopped and offers a spite check before resigning.

24.♕xg8+ ♚xg8 0-1

Let's examine one more game with ...♘d7 and see if White can find another way to lose! A little side note if you want to impress your friends: you can tell them you are studying the Sicilian Defense Dragon Variation, Yugoslav Attack Sosonko Variation. The move ...♘d7 constitutes the Sosonko, not that you need to know that in order to play good moves.

Game 3

Marinova, Elka (2075) – Velcheva, Maria (2160) [B77]
Bulgarian Women's Team Chp, Bankia 1992

1.e4 c5 2.♘c3 ♘c6 3.♘ge2 g6 4.d4 cxd4 5.♘xd4 ♗g7 6. ♗e3 ♘f6 7.♗c4 d6 8.f3 0-0 9.♕d2 ♘d7 10.♘xc6

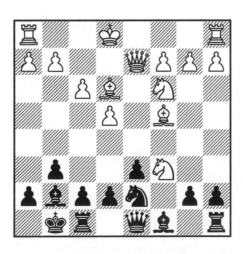

In this game, White decides to foil the dancing knights and double domination of c4 by trading a pair of horses on c6.

10...bxc6 11.♗h6 ♘e5 12.♗b3 ♗xh6 13.♕xh6 ♗e6 14.h4 ♗xb3 15.axb3 f6

Having taken care of the tandem knight attack, White is free to try her hand at running in with ♗h6 and force an exchange. Don't forget, had she not exchanged knights at c6, the d4-knight would be hanging as previously mentioned. White is all happy with herself, eliminating a pair of knights and applying pressure to the black king. White is so proud of her work that she incorrectly believes that Black played ...f7-f6 simply to create an escape square for her king!

16.h5? g5!

Now here is a unique idea: trapping the queen!

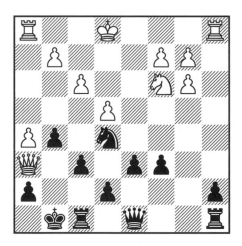

17.♖a6 ♘f7 18.♕xf8+ ♔xf8 19.♖xc6 ♕a5 0-1

White realizes it's over and tosses in a forlorn rook sortie to chop a pawn before resigning.

Now that we've played over a few games with 9...♘d7, give it a go yourself. Go online, fire up some speed games, and see how it works out for you. Try to replicate some of the themes, like controlling the c4 square with the knight duo! Use this new idea as an opportunity to expand your chess toolbox.

Game 4

Santo-Roman, Marc – Sosonko, Gennadi [B77]
Cannes Team G/60, 1992

1.e4 c5 2.♘f3 d6 3.d4 cxd4 4.♘xd4 ♘f6 5.♘c3 g6 6.♗e3 ♗g7 7.f3 ♘c6 8.♕d2 0-0 9.♗c4 ♘d7 10.h4 ♘b6 11.♗b3 ♘a5 12.♕d3 ♘xb3 13.axb3 d5 14.♘db5?!

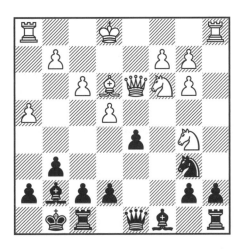

Ljubojević–Georgiev, Manila Interzonal 1990, saw the safer option of 14.♘de2 holding on to a solid center in classical style. Play continued 14...♗e6 15.0-0-0 dxe4 16.♕xe4 ♕c7 17.♘d4 ♗d7 18.h5, when the position was about equal. If you noticed that White could steal a pawn with 18.♕xe7, you are correct – however, after 18... ♖ae8, Black gets a little development going and the game is still virtually equal.

14...a6 15.♗xb6 ♕xb6 16.♘xd5

This is a wonderful position for the amateur chessplayer to study. On the surface, Black's position appears shaky; in reality, White has only a slight advantage. When you are faced with a situation where you sense that your opponent's forces are about to overrun your army, take a deep breath and rein in your emotions and the fear of losing – don't let it take control. White has a powerful knight attacking c7 and the black queen is under attack at b6, yet – after a queen retreat – what is White really doing? He has a hanging pawn at b2 to deal with, and his knights are easily pushed back. Let us not forget, too, that Black has the two bishops.

16...♛d8 17.♞bc3

White realizes that after moves like 17.♞dc7 ♜b8 18.♛xd8 ♜xd8, his advantage is gone. So if you can't go forward, retreat!

17...b5

Black is expanding and is quickly erasing White's minor edge conferred by the first move of the game. It should be noted that although 18.♞xb4 wins the pawn and Black can't recapture because of his rook at a8, this plan is still a waste of time for White: his own pawn is hanging at b2 and it is far better to complete development here than it is to chase pawns.

18.0-0-0 e6

Black is very close to turning the tables!

19.♞b4 ♛a5

Black's move indicates that he thinks he has the advantage. I'm not sure that's really true here; better is the simple 19...♝b7.

20.♞ca2

White uses his knights to prevent the enemy queen from reaching the back rank. My simple objection to this idea is that it looks artificial. Have you ever seen a Sicilian where White has tried this? Well... there is a reason rarely played ideas are rarely played and typically it's because they don't end well. There is no immediate threat, so 20.♞c6 is very playable here.

20...♗b7 21.♕d7 ♖ab8 22.♔b1 ♖fd8 23.♕e7 ♕b6 24.h5

One of the most difficult things in chess is deciding whether to paint your house or to go on vacation. Everyone loves a vacation and the opportunity to put your life on hold while you explore new and exciting things. Yet while you are on vacation the sun rises, the winds blow, and the rains come. If you house is not prepared to stand on its own, you may receive a very unpleasant surprise. That question is at the very heart of the Dragon: as each side tries to crush the enemy king, is his own home ready to withstand the elements? White played the vacation move 24.h5, whereas 24.♘d3 would be the "let's paint the walls" move.

24...gxh5 25.♕g5

Even here, I would have preferred 25.♘d3 to eliminate Black's counterplay.

25...h6 26.♕xh5 ♖xd1+ 27.♖xd1 ♖d8 28.♘d3?!

Better to exchange rooks and then play ♘d3: 28.♖xd8+ ♕xd8 29.♘d3, with an edge for White.

28...a5 29.♖e1??

The game is about equal with 29.b4 a4 30.♘c3 ♗c6 31.e5.

29...♖xd3 30.cxd3 ♕f2 0-1

White found the worst move on the board with 29.♖e1 and was quickly punished.

Game 5

Estrin, Yakov – Voronkov, Boris
Moscow Chp 1956

1.e4 c5 2.♘f3 d6 3.d4 cxd4 4.♘xd4 ♘f6 5.♘c3 g6 6.♗e3 ♗g7 7.f3 ♘c6 8.♕d2 0-0 9.♗c4 ♘d7 10.0-0-0

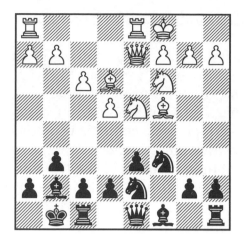

10...♞b6

Chess is full of little esthetic delights and White's c4-bishop provides Black great joy when it is kicked back to b3.

11.♗b3 ♞e5 12.♕e2

Dragon players: note that White loves his dark-squared bishop almost as much as Black does. Hence, we should view the purpose of 12.♕e2 mainly as preserving the bishop, and controlling c4 as happenstance. If that's the case, then we do not know yet if White will go all-out on the kingside or try to hold the fort on the queenside.

12...♗d7 13.f4 ♗g4 14.♞f3 ♞xf3

Confronted with the prospect of dropping an exchange, White prefers to retreat the knight and let the pawns be doubled.

15.gxf3 ♗d7

A worthy option is 15...♗e6. This is a very thematic idea in the Dragon, where if White exchanges on e6 the doubled pawns take away the d5 square from the knight. Novices fear that the e6-pawn will make for an easy target, but practice over many games has shown otherwise.

16.h4 a5

We frequently see an eye-for-an-eye approach in the Dragon: White thrusts on the kingside and Black's best play is often to thrust back on the queenside. The best defense in a Dragon is often a counterattack. This is not a line for timid players!

17.♘d5?

White wants to exchange knights in order to slow down Black's attack and to give more scope to his own bishops. What was said about the previous move and Black's fear also applies to White. This is a very common mistake – failing to commit fully to the attack and letting fate decide the outcome. Here, if White ignores his bishop and goes all out, he comes close to a knockout: 17.h5 a4 18.hxg6 axb3 19.gxh7+ ♚h8 20.cxb3 ♕c7 21.♔b1 f5 22.♖dg1 ♖f7 23.♕g2, and his attack is virtually winning!

17...♘xd5 18.♗xd5 e6 19.♗c4 b5

White preserves his bishop at the expense of tempo after tempo. Now Black's position has gone from potentially lost to a slight advantage.

20.♗d3 h5?

Slowing down White. However, 20...♕f6! would slow White down by attacking.

21.♔b1 a4 22.a3

A classic mistake: the a3-pawn becomes a target. A good maxim (taken slightly out of context here) is that, "a premature attack on the wing is best countered with an attack in the center." Black's attack is not really premature but the counter in the center with 22.e5 should be strongly considered.

22...b4 23.axb4 a3

White's kingside is about to be hit by a storm.

24.c3 axb2 25.♕xb2 ♕c7 26.♖c1 ♖a4

It's hard to find a defense for White – possibly 27.f5 creating some counter on the kingside while waiting to see if Black will double his rooks or go ...♖b8 or ...♕b7. White is not lost yet, so it's worth a shot at counterplay.

27.♔c2

The attempt to run away makes Black's choice very clear.

27...♖fa8! 28.♖a1?

Oddly enough, running back with 28.♔b1 is a better option.

28...♗xc3 29.♕xc3 ♖a2+ 0-1

A crushing finish.

Game 6

Bosboom, Manuel (2365) – Riemersma, Li (2395) [B77]
Dutch Team Chp 1987

1.e4 c5 2.♘f3 d6 3.d4 cxd4 4.♘xd4 ♘f6 5.♘c3 g6 6.♗e3 ♗g7 7.f3 0-0 8.♕d2 ♘c6 9.♗c4 ♘d7 10.0-0-0 ♘b6 11.♗b3 ♘a5

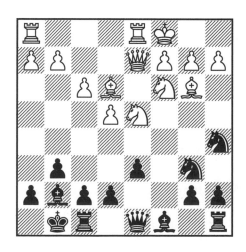

In the previous game, Black played 11...♘e5 eyeing the c4 square. 11...♘a5 is another route to the same square, with the additional option of capturing the b3-bishop. The trade-off with ...♘c6-a5 is that here the knight is less centrally placed, whereas ...♘e5 exerts pressure on f3 and that's often a critical factor. Let us also remember the maxim, "knights on the rim are dim;" however, if you know you are going to move to c4 or to take at b3 then this is a fine move.

12.♕e2

The prophylactic 12.♕e2 is a smarter option than charging the h-pawn, as Black is fine after 12.h4 ♘bc4 13.♗xc4 ♘xc4 14.♕e2 ♘xe3 15.♕xe3 h5.

12...♗d7 13.♔b1 ♖c8 14.♘d5

14.♘d5 prematurely releases the tension in the center and facilitates a clear plan of attack for Black. A better option is to proceed with 14.h4.

14...♘xb3 15.♘xb3 ♘xd5 16.♖xd5 ♗e6

Black's strong bishops rake the queenside, providing a slight edge.

17.♖g5

Here 17.♖d2 is virtually forced, as now there are multiple ways to punish White. 17...♗f6 18.♖g3 ♗h4 trapping the rook is one way. Black goes instead for the knockout, leaving the rook on an awkward square.

17...a5 18.h4 a4 19.♘d4 ♗c4 20.♕f2 e5!

A player who musters up the courage to block in the Dragon bishop always deserves an exclamation point. You might be surprised to learn that this is a theme in many Dragon positions. Here it's a clear warning to White that Black intends to do serious damage.

21.♘e2 d5 22.h5 h6 23.♖g4 d4 24.♗c1

White retreats the bishop to c1 as he has no faith in the tricky idea of hxg6; he most likely came to terms with 24.hxg6 dxe3 25.♕xe3 ♖c6 26.gxf7+ ♖xf7, when Black is very strong. However, he misses the point that he's dead lost after Black's next move and the "tricks" at least provide some small degree of hope.

24...♗e6 25.♖gh4 g5 26.♖4h2 f5

White must now come to terms with the fact that he's totally shut down and all his pieces are on the kingside, with none of them offering any support to his now-helpless king.

27.♘g3 f4 28.♘f1 ♕d7 29.g4 d3

The little d-pawn rips White's hopes apart like a zipper. A steady hand would play 30.c3 here, but what White offers as a defense is almost a helpmate.

30.b3? axb3 31.axb3 ♗xb3?

Black returns the favor, missing 31...dxc2+ 32.♔b2 ♕d3 33.♕b6 ♕c3+ 34.♔a2 ♖a8+ 35.♗a3 ♖xa3+ 36.♔xa3 ♖a8+ 37.♕a7 ♖xa7#!

32.c3? ♗c2+ 0-1

White overlooked the simple 32.cxb3 ♖c2 33.♕b6! when, although he is still behind, there are no forced mates.

White Doesn't Play 9.♗c4; Transpositions

I will not go too deeply into the theory, as our focus in this book is to recognize patterns and develop a natural approach to the opening. However, I would be completely remiss if I did not take a little detour here. The next several ideas we will look at involve games where White plays 9.0-0-0 instead of 9.♗c4. You may ignore the position below and just play any move as if White had played 9.♗c4. By doing so, you allow White to steer back toward the mainline Dragon with 10.♗c4.

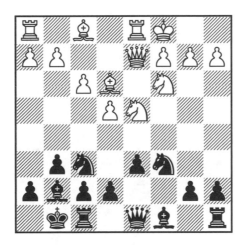

Position after 9.0-0-0 instead of 9.♗c4

A few pages back, I offered the general suggestion that you refrain from trying to figure how to punish move-order deviations over the board. Let me be clear: I'm giving you not only permission, but the strong suggestion that if White plays 9.0-0-0 instead of 9.♗c4, you can use that as an opportunity to explore moves like 9...♘xd4 or 9...d5, which we will cover soon.

While I think it's bad to try to punish or refuting move-order deviations, I also think it's foolish to totally ignore them. Ignoring the precise move order will rob you of the opportunity to develop one of the most important skills you can acquire in chess – a skill which is so important, yet which many players below master level are not even aware of. Let's take a quick side-trip to examine this critical skill called *transposition*.

Transposition

"Transposition" is an order of moves (move sequence) that results in a position which can also be obtained by another and usually more common sequence of moves. The term is reserved almost exclusively for the discussion of opening transpositions. Astute players will use transposition to avoid difficult opening lines and to bait their opponents into positions that are unfamiliar and difficult to play. In the words of the former heavyweight boxing champion Larry Holmes, he's taken his opponents out into deep water and drowned them. When you hear players referring to "transpose" as a verb, they mean taking the game to a different opening line from which it started.

Consider this position:

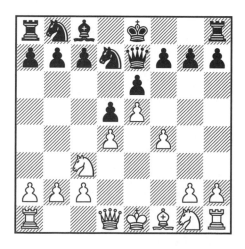

Can you name this opening? Can you demonstrate the move order to reach this position? I hope that by now you'll not be surprised to learn there is more than one correct answer.

The most common way to get here is via the Steinitz Variation of the French Defense: 1.e4 e6 2.d4 d5 3.♘c3 ♘f6 4.♗g5 ♗e7 5.e5 ♘fd7 6.♗xe7 ♕xe7 7.f4.

Pretend for a moment that the French Defense is your wheelhouse, your true-blue defense against 1.e4. What if your opponent opens with 1.d4 and launches a Trompowsky Attack? If you can transpose into a French Defense, you would have an advantage in preparation, right? This could happen with the following move order: 1.d4 ♘f6 2.♗g5 e6 3.e4 ♗e7 4.♘c3 d5 5.e5 ♘fd7 6.♗xe7 ♕xe7 7.f4. Same position, but different opening moves.

To give a different example, here we have a Nimzo-Indian Defense: 1.d4 ♘f6 2.c4 e6 3.♘c3 ♗b4 4.e3 0-0 5.♗d3 c5 6.♘f3 cxd4 7.exd4 d5 8.0-0 dxc4 9.♗xc4 ♘c6 10.a3 ♗e7.

And this, my friend, is a Caro-Kann Defense: 1.e4 c6 2.d4 d5 3.exd5 cxd5 4.c4 ♘f6 5.♘c3 e6 6.♘f3 ♗b4 7.♗d3 dxc4 8.♗xc4 0-0 9.0-0 ♘c6 10.a3 ♗e7.

Indeed, they are the same position. There's no diagram, as I want you to play it out on a board so that you truly get the idea.

It's not simply about ending up in the same position via different move orders. It can also take the shape of persuading your opponent to play along with you in a given direction. Imagine taking a scrap of paper about the size of your thumbnail and, without being noticed, trying to blow softly to move it across a table.

The average tournament player can easily overlook the nuances of using transpositions. During the Philadelphia International way back in 1984, GM Dmitry Gurevich recommended that I stop playing the Modern Benoni with the move order 1.d4 ♘f6 2.c4 c5 because it allowed the Taimanov Attack (7.f4), which at the time was just crushing Black. He suggested that I simply substitute ...e7-e6 on move two (1.d4 ♘f6 2.c4 e6) to increase the chances that White would play 3.♘f3 in order to avoid the Nimzo-Indian (3.♘c3 ♗b4), when with the knight on f3 the option of playing the Taimanov line is now off the table.

This was subtle in the sense that I threatened a Nimzo-Indian, which at the time was generally avoided, and therefore transposed into a line of the Benoni without having to face the most challenging line of the day. Alternatively, our approach can be brutal, as in our next chapter where we immediately seek to punish White for failing to play 9.♗c4.

Chapter 2

///

9.0-0-0 ♘xd4

Playing this early knight trade has shock value against a novice player. "Hey, you took my knight! Should I be able to refute this early knight exchange?" This is followed by complete confusion for a few moves, and finally the players settle back into a game of chess. Well, we can hope that is their reaction, right?

Full disclosure: you can play 9...♘xd4 against 9.♗c4 or 9.0-0-0, but it's most effective against 9.0-0-0, and that will be the focus here. Let's look at some games and see if we can pick up some patterns and concepts.

Game 7

Ostermeyer, Peter (2200) – Sosonko, Gennadi (2470) [B76]
West German Chp, Mannheim 1975

Did you catch the joke in the selection of this game? The very first game where we are reviewing the idea of ...♘c6xd4, the black pieces are being played by Sosonko, the same player after whom the ...♘d7 line is named. I'm sure he would have jumped at the chance to play ...♘d7 in this game too, but because White has played 9.0-0-0 instead of 9.♗c4, he takes a different path. If you think about it, what's the sense of relocating a knight to d7 to go to b6 in order to attack a bishop that's not at c4 yet?

1.e4 c5 2.♘f3 d6 3.d4 cxd4 4.♘xd4 ♘f6 5.♘c3 g6 6.♗e3 ♗g7 7.f3 ♘c6 8.♕d2 0-0 9.0-0-0 ♘xd4

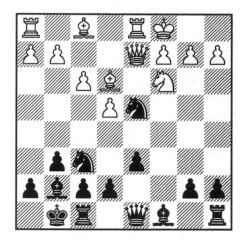

This is our bold starting position where we yell at White to wake up! Not to be repetitious, but let's not forget Mr. 9...♘d7. Sosonko would have played 9...♘d7 against 9. ♗c4, so just keep that in mind.

10.♗xd4 ♗e6

Do you see the idea? What do you want to do in many Dragon lines? That's right, challenge and fight for the c4 square. In this case, since White delayed ♗c4 we take control first with ...♗e6. Very cool idea, huh?

11.♔b1 ♛c7 12.g4 ♖fc8 13.h4 ♛a5

Remember, our goal here is to learn patterns and ideas, not to memorize lines. Normally you might overlook moves like this because the book says they are "normal," but we want to understand the ideas and concepts so we can use them in other positions. Did you notice anything odd here? Are you wondering why Black moved his queen twice? Was that a mistake? Well, if you thought about that, then great! If you missed it, that's OK too. It just means you trust GMs and book authors too much! And no, it was not a mistake. Had Black played ...♛d8-a5 on move 11, White would have uncorked

12.♘d5!. So we'd have something like this: 11...♛a5 12.♘d5 ♛xd2 13.♘xe7+ ♚h8 14.♖xd2 a6 15.c3 ♖fe8 16.♗xf6 ♗xf6 17.♘d5, when White has a very nice game. Pulling it all together, the reason we stop the queen on c7 on move 11 is because we want to get the rook safely to c8, and then after we play 12...♖fc8, we can get on with taking the queen to a5 on move 13 because now the idea of ♘c3-d5 would be a complete failure due to 14.♘d5 ♛xd2 15.♘xe7+ ♚f8 16.♖xd2 ♚xe7. This is a theme in many Dragon lines where ...♛xd2 comes without check, White tosses in the *intermezzo* ♘xe7+ and the black king simply moves back toward the knight.

14.a3 ♖ab8

Black has his rooks all lined up and ready to start the attack. No need to worry about getting them set, as they are already good to go. White is ahead in the pawn-shoving game, but Black is ahead in lining up his cannons!

15.h5 b5 16.h6 ♗h8 17.♗xf6 ♗xf6 18.♘d5 b4

Black avoids the queen exchange and takes the opportunity to shove his pawns forward.

19.axb4 ♛a4 20.b5

White must play 20.♘xf6+ in order to remove the powerful bishop. The pawn moves on the queenside only advance Black's plans. Better is 20.♘xf6+ exf6 21.c4 ♖c6 22.♖c1 ♖xb4 23.♛d4.

20...♗xd5 21.exd5 a6 0-1

White is in a world of trouble and the position cannot be saved. However, this is a slightly premature resignation. He should make Black demonstrate a winning line, for example 22.g5 axb5 23.gxf6 ♖a8 24.c4 bxc4 25.♛d4 ♛a2+ 26.♚c2 c3 27.♚d3 cxb2.

Game 8

Pustelny-Conrad, Dieter – Sehner, Norbert [B76]
Bochum (Germany) 1979

The following game was played twice between masters: John Hall and William Watson made the exact same moves to an identical end in the 1979 British Championship.

1.e4 c5 2.♘f3 d6 3.d4 cxd4 4.♘xd4 ♘f6 5.♘c3 g6 6.♗e3 ♗g7 7.f3 0-0 8.♕d2 ♘c6 9.0-0-0 ♘xd4

We have the same move order and position as our previous game. Our game stays on the same track until move 11 when White deviates.

10.♗xd4 ♗e6

Again, Black takes control of the c4 square by planting his own bishop at e6. Makes sense, right? How can White control c4 now?

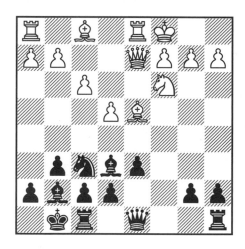

11.♘d5 ♗xd5

White tries to control c4 by planting his knight in and cutting the scope of Black's bishop. Black agrees, and chops off the knight to increase his control of the c-file.

12.exd5 ♖c8 13.h4 ♕c7

White has a clear plan to storm the kingside. but he overlooks one tiny problem.

14.h5 ♝h6!! 0-1

Crash, bang, *boom!* White overlooked a common pattern of ...♝g7-h6 pinning the queen to the king. Yes, that's what's going on; the queen is pinned and White can't break the pin by 15.♕xh6 because Black will mate with 15...♕xc2.

Regarding the basic pattern, in this case the bishop is unsupported. In other situations, Black will have played ...♘g4 or ...♕f8 supporting the bishop. This pin can be devastating and easy for White to overlook.

Game 9

Ziska, Bogi – Jakobsen, Peter [B76]
Aarhus Open, Denmark 1989

1.e4 c5 2.♘f3 d6 3.d4 cxd4 4.♘xd4 ♘f6 5.♘c3 g6 6.♝e3 ♝g7 7.f3 0-0 8.♕d2 ♘c6 9.0-0-0 ♘xd4 10.♝xd4 ♝e6

Reaching the same position as in our previous games. If ...♘xd4 is not to your liking, then no worries – there are other options that we will cover later. However, remember that the idea here is not to memorize opening lines or to get married to a variation: the goal of this book is to learn patterns and expose you to new ideas.

11.h4 ♕a5

In Game 4, Sosonko's queen stopped on c7 to have a cup of tea before flying off to a5. In this game, Black plays ...♕d8-a5 in one stroke. The difference from that earlier game is that there White played 11.♔b1 so that, had Black played 11...♕a5 immediately without stopping first on c7, White would have had the resource 12.♘d5! that we discussed in detail there. But, in the current position, if White uncorks 12.♘d5, Black takes the white queen at d2 with check and all is well with the world.

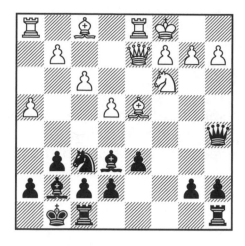

12.♔b1 ♖fc8

After White gets his king over to b1 and Black swings the f8-rook over to c8, the position is very similar to Game 7.

13.♘d5 ♕xd2

This is the primary fork in the road. In Game 7, White adopted a defensive approach with a2-a3. Here, White takes a different path and goes for simplification and a queen exchange.

14.♖xd2 ♗xd5 15.♗xf6 ♗xa2+

White could have held on to the pawn with the straightforward 15.exd5. White should be very careful, lest his desire to simplify become a series of small concessions that add up to a losing game. Take note of this point during your own games, as it's a common occurrence when playing "up," as the lower-rated player often is so happy to exchange pieces on what appears to be a near-equal footing, only to awake in an endgame and realize he is dead lost. I have seen this in countless games and at one time was guilty of this sin myself.

16.♔xa2 ♗xf6 17.c4 ♖c5

I deeply dislike White's last move, which plants a target for Black to attack. If you wave a flag in the bull's face, don't complain about the outcome. Having said that, is c5 really the best place for Black's rook? It's very committing and on intuition alone you have to wonder if White will ever have the move b2-b4, kicking the rook? 17...♖c6 would have worked just as well for the intended purpose.

18.♖d5 ♖ac8

White is playing into Black's plans by finding his own awkward squares for his rook. Strategically, the plan of g2-g3 with the threat of ♗h3, attacking the c8 square, may have more merit. Yet it is complicated, as it leaves the c4-pawn undefended and Black may harass the king with ...♖a4+.

19.h5

There is no justification for a kingside attack. The queens are off the board and White should defend. White is giving Black a free move to continue to attack the weakness created on c4 and in turn the queenside as a whole.

19...♖xd5

Black exchanges in order to break the center bind and penetrate White's defenses.

20.exd5

Capturing with the c pawn-allows 20...♖c2, winning.

20...b5

Busting the queenside open. It's not about the pawn count – it is all about activating pieces.

21.hxg6 hxg6 22.b3 bxc4 23.♗xc4

White must recapture with the bishop, else after the pawn re-capture Black penetrates with ...♖b8 rendering White defenseless: 23.bxc4 ♖b8 24.g3 ♖b2+ 25.♔a3 ♖f2 26.f4 ♖f3+ and the kingside falls apart.

23...♖c5 24.♔a3?

White activates his king, failing to understand how fragile his position is.

24...♗c3!

Back in my teens, when we played speed chess we would follow up sharp moves with random juvenile banter. This move would have warranted a "Ding dong, Avon calling!" Black threatens mate, leaving White with b3-b4 as the only move to create an escape square, which of course falls immediately to ...♖xc4 winning the bishop and the game's over.

25.♖c1 ♖a5# 0-1

Game 10

Mazi, Leon (2345) – Mencinger, Vojko (2390) [B76]
Finkenstein (Austria) 1995

1.e4 c5 2.♘f3 d6 3.d4 cxd4 4.♘xd4 ♘f6 5.♘c3 g6 6.f3 ♘c6 7.♗e3 ♗g7 8.♕d2 0-0 9.0-0-0 ♘xd4 10.♗xd4 ♗e6 11.♔b1 ♕c7

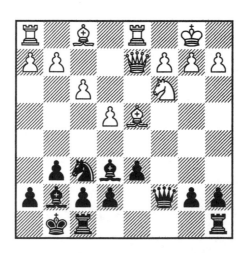

Had White played any move other than 11.♔b1, Black likely would have played 11...♕a5. However, as we've seen before, after 11.♔b1, 11...♕a5 meets with 12.♘d5!, when Black must retreat as he no longer exchanges on d2 with check. After 11.♔b1 ♕a5 12.♘d5 ♕d8 13.♗xf6 ♗xf6 14.♘xf6 exf6, Black's pawn structure is a mess and the d-pawn is hanging.

12.g4 ♖fc8 13.h4 ♕a5

Now ♘d5 is no longer feared: 14.♘d5 ♕xd2 15.♘xe7+ ♔f8 and White must take time to recapture the queen. This is why after ♔b1, Black must play ...♕c7 and ...♖fc8 in order to get the queen to a5.

14.a3 ♖ab8

Black is gearing up for an all-out assault on the white queenside. Notice that when White attacks the kingside he can leave his rook on h1, while when Black wants to attack White's queenside his queen rook must be played to b8 or c8: it very seldom serves a purpose on a8.

15.h5 b5 16.hxg6 hxg6 17.g5 b4

Black has two paths – the safer-looking 17...♘h5 or the text move 17...b4. The correct move is the aggressive ...b5-b4 as it keeps Black in the game. The timid ...♘h5 leads to a bad position for Black, for example 17...♘h5 18.♗xg7 ♔xg7 19.♗h3. This is sort of a refrain for the Dragon: the strong, aggressive path is usually the correct path.

18.♘b5 ♘h5 19.♗xg7 ♔xg7 20.♕d4+ ♔g8 21.axb4

White is too proud of his position here. The simple 21.♕xb4 ♕b6 22.♘d4 ♕xb4 23.axb4 ♖xb4 24.♘xe6 fxe6 25.♖d2 is a reasonable continuation. Instead, White allows counterchances that he will soon regret. That's good advice for a novice: learn to keep control of the game; play positions you understand; study and strive to learn those you don't.

21...♕a2+ 22.♔c1 ♗b3 23.♘a3 e5 24.♕d3 ♖xb4

Did White miss 22...♗b3? If not, did he really believe that the evaluation of this position was good for him? He is in a lot of trouble here.

25.♕a6 ♗e6

White attacks the rook, but with a little bishop retreat the b2-pawn is hanging and White is helpless to defend it (26.b3 ♖xb3).

26.♖xd6 ♕xb2+ 27.♔d1 ♕a1+ 28.♔d2 ♕c3+ 29.♔d1 ♕xf3+ 30.♔d2 ♖xe4 31.♗d3 ♕f4+ 0-1

Black's final moves are good enough for the full point. He could have teased White by allowing him to come within one move of mate, only to be mated first: 30...♘g3 31.♕xc8+ ♗xc8 32.♖d8+ ♔g7 33.♖dh8 ♘xf1+ 34.♔c1 ♕e3+ 35.♔d1 ♗g4#.

Game 11

Fierro Baquero, Martha Lorena (2205) – Hansen, Sune Berg (2505) [B76]
Úbeda (Spain) 1997

1.e4 c5 2.♘f3 d6 3.d4 cxd4 4.♘xd4 ♘f6 5.♘c3 g6 6.♗e3 ♗g7 7.f3 ♘c6 8.♕d2 0-0 9.0-0-0 ♘xd4 10.♗xd4 ♗e6 11.♔b1 ♕c7 12.h4

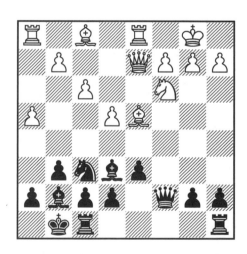

In our previous game, we saw 12.g4. Let's see where the idea of running the h-pawn up the board takes us. However, before we move on, please commit to memory as mentioned many times before: after ♔b1, we can only play ...♕d8-a5 after first moving ...♖fc8.

12...♖fc8 13.h5 ♕a5

Here Black would be better off playing 13...♘xh5. Yes, I'm aware that I advocated for going fast and strong, but notice that Black's rook is still on a8 and he has yet to establish any useful deployment against the white king. Where White has pushed his h-pawn twice, Black must take care not to fall behind.

14.hxg6 hxg6 15.♗d3 b5

This is a tricky spot for White. Should he play 16.♗xb5 to eliminate the pawn? The downside to that move is that Black plays 16...♖ab8 and takes the semi-open file. Should White play 16.a3, though, Black could push 16...b4. Yet this is possibly the best defense: 16.a3 b4 17.♘a2 ♗xa2 18.♔xa2, when White should be able to hold the position.

16.♕g5 ♖xc3 17.♗xc3 ♕xa2+

Notice how the previous game also featured ...♕xa2+. It's common on both sides of the Dragon for themes to appear over and over again. It's similar to doing a puzzle: you'll start to remember the shapes and patterns, and you just need to determine "does this piece fit here?" before actually moving the puzzle piece. If you start to think in that way you'll be adding lots of tools to your toolbox.

18.♔c1 b4 19.♗d4 ♖c8

Black correctly bears down on the white king. Often, novice Dragon players will see ghosts and defend when they should be attacking. But take a moment and look at the black king. Note that the black knight protects h7 and the black bishop protects h8 and h6. So, what if White chops off the f6-knight? The answer is pretty simple: we can recapture with the e7-pawn, which creates an escape square for the king. As dangerous as it might seem (and sometimes it is), often the case is that everything is holding together very nicely and players of the black pieces should trust The Force.

20.e5

Pushing the pawn ads no value to White's position. As the bishop controls more useful squares on d4 than on e5, forcing an exchange that places the bishop on e5 seems like a waste of time. Possibly White is considering sacrificing his light-squared bishop on g6 and wants to clear some space for a last-ditch attack. I don't see it but it's hard to justify White's plan. Better is 20.♕e3, with the idea of abandoning the queenside with ♔d2 and scampering away to safety.

20...dxe5 21.♗xe5 b3

Final chance to escape with 22.♔d2. It's not that White has any good moves, but that running with the king may avoid mate and allow White to live long enough to get back in the game should Black err.

22.♗c3 ♖xc3

Black sacrificed the exchange for active play on move 16. Only rarely do we see double exchange sacrifices, and when they do occur they can only mean one thing: lights out.

23.bxc3 ♘d5 24.♗xg6 fxg6

White plays his idea of sacrificing at g6, but at this point it's clearly an act of utter desperation.

25.♕xg6 ♕a1+ 26.♔d2 ♕xc3+ 27.♔c1 ♕e3+ 0-1

White resigns in view of 28.♔b1 bxc2+ 29.♕xc2 (29.♔xc2 ♕c3+ 30.♔b1 ♕b2#) 29...♘c3+ 30.♕xc3 ♕xc3 31.♖d8+ ♔f7 32.♖b8 ♕d2, and the dual mate threat of ...♗f5# or ...♗a2# cannot be stopped.

Game 12

Ruiz González, Guillermo (2309) – Molander, Riku (2234) [B76]
Budapest First Saturday #9, 1999

A very short game with a big surprise. Move orders matter, and White is punished quickly for an "innocent" mistake.

1.e4 c5 2.♘f3 d6 3.d4 cxd4 4.♘xd4 ♘f6 5.♘c3 g6 6.♗e3 ♗g7 7.f3 0-0 8.♕d2 ♘c6 9.0-0-0 ♘xd4 10.♗xd4 ♗e6 11.♔b1 ♕c7 12.h4 ♖fc8

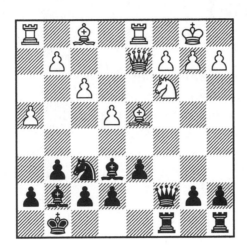

A very normal position; how can White engineer a disaster so quickly?

13.h5 ♕a5 14.♗xf6?? ♖xc3!

Ignoring the threat on a2, White failed to play a2-a3. Black's sharp eye enabled him to avoid the trap of playing by rote to reach a familiar position. A common mistake for novice players is not being fully present early in the opening phase. Add this one to your toolbox: yes, leaving a2 undefended is horrible here.

15.♕xc3

The obvious gain of the rook with 15.♗xc3 is met by 15...♕xa2+ and 16...♕a1#.

15...♕xa2+ 16.♔c1 ♗h6+ 0-1

Chapter 3

9.g4 ♘xd4

Let's look at a few games where White tries an early kingside attack with 9.g4. In this variation, we are presented with another opportunity to play 9...♘xd4, and in many lines we need to be aware that transpositions can occur. Don't worry about memorizing every line that could transpose; just be of the mindset that it's possible and over time, as your knowledge builds, your ability to see them and navigate them will increase.

Game 13

Pichler, Jürgen (2325) – Hofstetter, Hans-Joachim [B76]
Nuremberg Open 1987

1.e4 c5 2.♘f3 d6 3.d4 cxd4 4.♘xd4 ♘f6 5.♘c3 g6 6.♗e3 ♗g7 7.f3 0-0 8.♕d2 ♘c6 9.g4

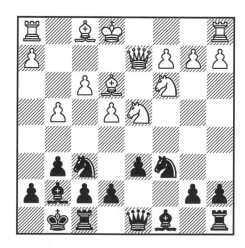

Moving pawns aggressively before castling or completing minor-piece development leads me to believe that my opponent is willing to take chances and storm the king. There is a maxim in chess that says a premature attack on the wing should be countered in the center. Whether it applies here or not is a question for opening theory, but it's always good to remember these little mantras, as they can help you to focus on areas of the board and to see ideas you might otherwise overlook.

9...♘xd4 10.♗xd4 ♗e6 11.0-0-0 ♛a5

Continuing with our theme of exchanging knights in the center and playing ...♗e6 controlling the c4 square, Black goes for the early ...♛a5 idea. As in previous games, we need to take into account whether the white king sits on c1 or b1. That is an important trigger in deciding how to go about positioning our pieces for the attack.

12.a3

I'm not a fan of White's castling long and then voluntarily moving the queenside pawns. If you are forced to do so to stop a threat, that's fine. But doing it for free provides targets, and Black wastes no time in lining his rook up to attack. I much prefer the simple 12.♔b1.

12...♖ab8 13.h4 b5 14.♘d5 ♛xd2+ 15.♖xd2 ♗xd5

It is slightly better here for Black to recapture with the knight, e.g. 15...♘xd5 16.exd5 ♗d7 17.♗xa7 ♖a8 18.♗d4 b4 19.♗xg7 ♔xg7 20.♖d3 ♖a5 21.♖e3 bxa3 22.bxa3 e5 23.dxe6 ♗xe6, and White's a-pawn will fall. As a general rule, we favor bishops over knights, and if for that alone I would go with 15...♘xd5.

16.exd5 ♖b7

An odd move without purpose; rooks should not be defending pawns against bishops. Better is the simple and straightforward 16...a5.

17.h5? ♗h6 0-1

Our "sneaky bishop" pattern pops up again. Notice how this was never an option early on because of g4-g5, while now without the pawn on h4 to support g5, it's simply a hideous blunder.

Game 14

Sebastianelli, Diego – Hugony, Fabrizio [B76]
San Benedetto Open 1989

1.e4 c5 2.♘f3 d6 3.d4 cxd4 4.♘xd4 ♘f6 5.♘c3 g6 6.♗e3 ♗g7 7.f3 ♘c6 8.♕d2 0-0 9.g4 ♘xd4 10.♗xd4 ♗e6 11.0-0-0 ♕a5 12.♔b1

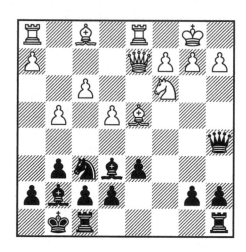

In the previous game, White played 12.a3, so now that White has played the "better" move, let's see how well he performs.

12...♖fc8

The question in many positions is often, "which rook?" Fortunately, when playing the Dragon it's almost always the f8-rook. Our discussion in Game 7 demonstrated how powerful ♘c3-d5 can be and how having the f8 square free helps Black, as he can answer ♘xe7+ with ...♔f8. If you are unsure as to what that means, review Game 7 and its notes again. It's an important pattern that you must not forget.

13.h4? ♖xc3

White completely missed this, otherwise he would have played the safer and sounder move 13.a3. Ironically, if he were an astute student of the game he would have known about Russian GM Vladimir Simagin who played this crushing move against GM Alatortsev in the 1943 Moscow Championship. While pawns generally provide better protection to the king on their original squares, here it was necessary due to the threats against a2.

14.♕xc3 ♕xa2+ 15.♔c1 ♗xg4

This is the first time we've seen the bone-cracking sacrifice (of bishop or knight) on g4. This is a dangerous tactical theme that you should look to add to your toolbox. You'll find that it rips away the f-pawn, leaving the e-pawn ripe for the picking. However, in other cases the virtue of having a knight on g4 plays out by supporting forks galore or supporting a sneaky Dragon bishop on h6.

This capture must have struck fear into White. However, chess is a game of calm nerves and a steady hand. It's far from over for the first player, and careful play can bring him back to an even game. One false move, though, and it's over.

The straightforward approach is 16.fxg4 ♕a1+ 17.♔d2 ♘xe4+ 18.♔e1 ♘xc3 (the natural impulse to play 18...♕xd1+ is wrong; a good study session is to play out the lines after 18...♘xc3 and the lines resulting from 18...♕xd1+) 19.♖xa1 ♗xd4 20.♗g2 ♘b5 21.♗xb7 ♖b8 22.♗c6 ♗xb2 23.♖a6 ♘d4 24.♔d2 ♘xc6 25.♖xc6 ♖b7. Black is better: 26.♖b8? ♗c3+ −+.

16.♕e3 e5 17.fxg4 ♘xg4 0-1

White resigns because of our thematic move ...♗g7-h6, which leads to the win of material and the game for Black. After 17.fxg4, did White assume that Black would capture the bishop on d4? It would explain not seeing the knockout punch, but the resulting position is still good for Black: 17...exd4 18.♕a3 (necessary; 18.♕xd4 ♘xg4 is crushing and forces 19.♕xg7+) 18...♕xa3 19.bxa3 ♘xg4.

Game 15

Shimanov, Aleksandr (2586) – Kabanov, Nikolai (2520) [B76]
Khanty-Mansiysk 2011

1.e4 c5 2.♘f3 d6 3.d4 cxd4 4.♘xd4 ♘f6 5.♘c3 g6 6.♗e3
♗g7 7.f3 0-0 8.♕d2 ♘c6 9.g4 ♘xd4 10.♗xd4 ♗e6 11.h4

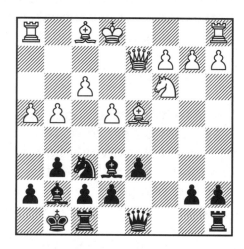

White leaves the king in the center so he can focus on applying maximum force against Black's kingside. Black should play sharply but be careful not to overreact or become desperate, for his position is fundamentally sound and sooner or later White must connect the rooks.

11...♕a5 12.h5 ♖fc8

Black's queen sortie clears the way for the king's rook and pins the knight to c3. White's position looks fierce, but even if White opens the h-file, swings the queen to h2, and checks on h7, Black can simply play ...♔f8. That takes a lot of time, and Black must only find modest plans on the queenside to slow White down.

13.♗e2 ♗c4 14.hxg6 hxg6 15.g5 ♘h5

There is no clear way for White to exploit this move. In the Dragon, you'll often be forced as Black to play ...♘f6-h5 when White will sac the exchange, giving up his rook for the knight to pry open his opponent's kingside. In this position, it leads to nothing. Notice the added benefit now of ...♛d8-a5, applying pressure to the g5-pawn and keeping White's queen tied down as its only defender.

16.♝xg7 ♚xg7 17.♝xc4 ♜xc4 18.0-0-0 ♜ac8

In theory, the position is equal, but only in the sense of a bowling ball balanced on a razor's edge. Dangerous play abounds for both sides. For example, 19.♜h2 ♛e5 20.♜dh1 b5 21.f4 ♛c5 22.♛e2 ♛d4 23.♜xh5 and it's still potentially equal!

19.♚b1 ♜xc3 20.bxc3 ♜xc3

Ironically, after the exchange sacrifice, Black is "more equal," while without it I dare say he would be "less equal."

21.♛d4+ e5 22.♛xd6 ♜c6 23.♜d5?? ♛b6+ 0-1

One fatal move spoils an interesting game. The motifs in this game (controlling c4 and sacrificing the exchange on c3) are very common and always worth keeping in mind.

Game 16

Piechota, Jan – Ciejka, Tadeusz [B76]
Polish Chp 1946

Polish players of the post-war era have slipped into the obscurity of chess history. What we do know is that this game was from the Polish individual national championship where participants are the best national players and from which the Polish chess federation would determine their Olympiad team.

1.e4 c5 2.♞f3 ♞c6 3.d4 cxd4 4.♞xd4 ♞f6 5.♞c3 d6 6.f3 g6 7.♝e3 ♝g7 8.♛d2 0-0 9.g4 ♞xd4 10.♝xd4 ♝e6 11.h4 ♛a5 12.♝e2

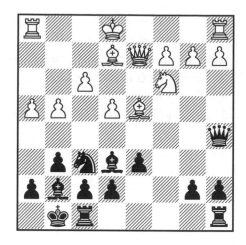

Instead of 12.♗e2, the previous game featured 12.h5, when GM Shimanov followed with aggressive play on the kingside and no attempt to slow Black down on the queenside. In this game, White takes a different approach and tries to attack while countering Black's attack.

12...♖ac8 13.a3 a6

This game could have easily transposed back to Game 15; however, the critical move 13.a3 sets the tone for alternating between attack and defense. The downside of this move is that Black, too, can toss in some defense with 13...h5!. But instead we find that Black passes up that chance and plays the perfunctory 13...a6, preparing his own queenside advance without regard for his king's safety.

14.h5 ♖fd8

This might appear to be an odd square for the rook. More often, in Dragon games you'll see Black attempt to double on the c-file or have the rooks use the squares c8 and b8 as their base camp. Those ideas are not dogma, however, and you'll find many games where Black plays ...♕d8-a5 and places the rook at d8. It's an idea to keep in mind, especially if you have never used it. Even from d8 the rook could travel to d7 and double on c7 – the possibilities are many. From d8, the rook supports the idea of a ...d6-d5 pawn break and, in this game, with the white king still in the center of the board, ...♖f8-d8 seems like a rational approach. Note that the rooks on the traditional squares of b8 and c8 support the plan of ...a7-a6 and then advancing with ...b7-b5. White could view this setup as an opportunity to immediately castle queenside before proceeding with his kingside attack.

15.hxg6 hxg6

White still must decide if he going to castle queenside, connecting his rooks, or go all in for the immediate attack and leave his king in the center.

16.♕e3 ♖c6

Stopping the threat of ♗d4-b6 and allowing Black to quickly double his rooks should the need arise.

17.♗d3 b5 18.b4?

White wants to relieve the pressure on c3 and stop the threat of ...b5-b4. All good ideas, and he could have accomplished this with 18.♔f2. Instead 18.b4 creates many holes and gives away the natural advantage that White enjoys from moving first.

18...♕c7

Now Black threatens the obvious ...♖xc3 and he is set to triple on the c-file.

19.♘e2 ♖c8 20.♔f2 ♗c4

Exerting pressure on the d3-bishop and thus weakening the c2 square.

21.♖ac1

White misses 21.g5, forcing the exchange of dark-squared bishops and providing an opportunity for White's remaining pieces to become active. Black's strong counter shuts out the dark-squared bishop and launches a powerful central break.

21...e5! 22.♗a1 d5!

After this, White should choose between 23.g5, creating tactical opportunities, or 23.♗xc4, hoping to simplify his way out of this mess.

23.♕g5

In lieu of the aforementioned options, White abandons the center, and for what purpose? Black's king is fairly safe and his own king is soon to be short of defenders.

23...dxe4 24.fxe4 ♕d8 25.♕h4

Many a novice overreacts to the queen and rook's being doubled against their king. Yet what is the threat here? Even if we take the f6-knight off the board, White can only penetrate to h7 with check, when Black simply walks away to f8.

25...♗xd3 26.cxd3 ♕xd3 27.♖cd1 ♕xe4

White's king is now naked and the temperature is about to drop below freezing.

28.g5 ♘g4+ 29.♔e1 ♖c2 30.♖h2 ♕f3 31.♕h7+ ♔f8 32.♕h3 ♖xe2+ 0-1

White must recapture with 33.♖xe2, which leaves his queen hanging; hence, resignation is in order. In the end, White got his silly check in at h7 and followed up with a losing move in a hopeless position.

Chapter 4

9.g4 ♗xg4

In Games 13-16, we examined 9...♘xd4 as a solid idea against 9.g4 and there is nothing lacking in that choice. However, putting everything on the line with 9...♗xg4 will force you to learn attacking themes and to play very aggressively, which will improve your overall skill set.

Game 17

Vaisman, Alexander – Gufeld, Eduard [B76]
Ukrainian Chp 1958

1.e4 c5 2.♘f3 d6 3.d4 cxd4 4.♘xd4 ♘f6 5.♘c3 g6 6.♗e3 ♗g7 7.f3 ♘c6 8.♕d2 0-0 9.g4 ♗xg4

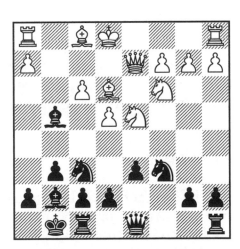

9...♘xd4 works well against just about any move that White can play. Even against 9.g4, Black has done just fine. However, you are a Dragon player, a chessboard pirate! You are a fighter who wants to win with bold moves and exciting combinations, creating art with your play. If that's who you are, you must add 9.g4 ♗xg4 to your arsenal.

This 1958 game was the first time 9...♗xg4 was played. It would be another 27 years (1985) before it made another appearance on the chess scene. That's very odd when you consider that the player of the black pieces is GM Gufeld, a Dragon expert who authored more than eighty chess books.

10.fxg4 ♘xg4

The immediate threat is for Black to play ...♘xe3 and follow up by taking the knight on d4. White must do something immediately to deal with that threat.

11.♘xc6

White has also tried 11.♗g1, which is not the best of options as it makes it very hard to castle queenside due to the threat of ...♗g7-h6, pinning the queen to the king (see the next three games). If not 11.♘xc6, then 11.♘b3 is the only other real move that White should consider in this position.

11...bxc6 12.♗e2 ♘xe3

Black is happy to take off the dark-squared bishop as that increases the power of his own bishop at g7. I prefer Black in this position as the h-pawn and the e-pawn are weak and don't contribute to the game. Black also has the semi-open b-file and solid attacking chances.

13.♕xe3 ♖b8 14.♖b1 ♕a5

White decides that he'd rather castle kingside than queenside – a bold choice, given that there is no immediate threat against the queenside and the kingside is virtually bare. Why not 14.0-0-0 e6 15.♗c4 d5 16.♗b3 ? – White seems to be OK here.

15.0-0 e6 16.a3 d5 17.♘d1 ♕a4

Placing the knight on d1 looks awkward. We can assume that it planned to gallop to the aid of the king. Now the immediate threat of ...♗g7-d4, winning the queen, will force White to rethink the knight's travel plans.

18.c4 ♖b3 19.♘c3 ♕a5 20.cxd5 cxd5 21.♗d1

White is obviously very uncomfortable with the pressure on c2 and b2, so he kicks the rook back. If Black wants to defy the bishop, he can play speculative lines like 21...d4 22.♕f2 dxc3 23.♗xb3 cxb2 24.♖xb2 ♕c3 25.♖d2 ♗h6 26.♖e2 ♕xb3 27.♕xa7. However, it's very dangerous to pursue these ideas when you are down a piece.

21...♖b7 22.♕f3?

The passive 22.♘a4 allows time for White to untangle and hold on to his material edge. The text move hands Black the victory.

22...♗xc3 23.exd5 exd5 24.b4 ♕xa3 25.♖b3 ♗d4+

This *intermezzo* check saves the pieces and leaves White completely lost.

26.♔h1 ♕a6 27.b5 ♕e6 28.♖d3 ♕e5 29.♕e2 ♖d8

No matter what White finds, Black has an answer.

30.♕d2 ♗c5 31.♗f3 ♖xb5 32.♗xd5 ♖b2 33.♕f4 ♖xd5 0-1

Yes, in the final position there is a check at f7, but after ...♔h8 Black still threatens mate at h2 and defending against it will cost more material.

Game 18

Psakhis, Lev (2585) – Tolnai, Tibor (2480) [B76]
Dortmund 1989

    1.e4 c5 2.♘f3 d6 3.d4 cxd4 4.♘xd4 ♘f6 5.♘c3 g6 6.♗e3 ♗g7 7.f3 0-0 8.♕d2 ♘c6 9.g4 ♗xg4 10.fxg4 ♘xg4 11.♗g1

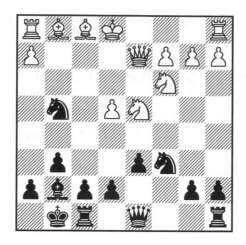

The result of this game after 11.♗g1 made 9...♗xg4 a very popular line.

11...e6 12.h4 h5

This move solidly anchors the knight on g4 and stops the advance of the h-pawn. Now White cannot castle queenside because of ...♗g7-h6.

13.♘xc6 bxc6 14.♗e2 ♗h6 15.♕d3 ♘e5 16.♕g3 ♖b8

Black has his cake and eats it too. He's saved the knight, taken control of the diagonal h6 to c1, kicked the opposing queen around, and grabbed the semi-open file.

17.b3 ♕a5 18.♖d1 ♗g7 19.♖xd6 ♖bd8

A twist of irony: this game appears as a diagram after 18...♗g7 in Gufeld's book, *Secrets of the Sicilian Dragon*. The ironic part? Gufeld doesn't share the opening moves, he does not take credit for creating this line, and he only discusses why 19.♖xd6? is a bad move. It would appear he kept the "Secrets of the Dragon" to himself. Gufeld recommended the "grovelly" 19.♔f1 over 19.♖xd6.

20.♖xd8 ♖xd8

9.g4 ♗xg4

White has exchanged his only active rook and is saddled with a rook trapped in the corner. As a result, White is down an active rook for the rest of the "playable" game.

21.♔f1 ♖d2 22.♖h3 ♘g4

White cannot capture the knight because his own knight at c3 would fall: 23.♗xg4 hxg4 24.♕xg4 ♗xc3 (or, if the rook retreats, still 24...♗xc3).

23.♕b8+ ♔h7 24.b4 ♕a3

Black keeps the pressure on the knight. I give credit to White for finding resourceful play in a very bad position.

25.♕xa7 ♕c1+

Not resourceful enough, though. Black penetrates to the back rank and moves in for the kill.

26.♔g2 ♗xc3 27.♖xc3 ♖xe2+

White put a lot of effort with ♕b8, b3-b4, and ♕xa7 all to save the knight – and in the end it's the bishop on e2 that falls. White can resign here.

28.♔g3 ♕e1+ 29.♔f3 ♕f1+ 30.♔g3 0-1

White surrendered after realizing he's mated after 30...♖g2+ 31.♔h3 ♖xg1#.

Game 19

Gurevich, Ilya (2495) – Pelikian, Jefferson (2255) [B76]
World U26 Team Chp, Maringa (Brazil) 1991

1.e4 c5 2.♘f3 d6 3.d4 cxd4 4.♘xd4 ♘f6 5.♘c3 g6 6.♗e3 ♗g7 7.f3 0-0 8.♕d2 ♘c6 9.g4 ♗xg4 10.fxg4 ♘xg4 11.♗g1 e6 12.♘f3

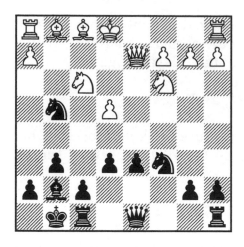

As in the previous game, White plays 11.♗g1 and ends in failure. This game features a 240-point upset by the 26-year-old Brazilian master Jefferson Pelikian, who defeats the World Junior Champion, 19-year-old GM Ilya Gurevich. Regarding White's last move, while 12.♘f3 is playable, it's not clear what use it will be on f3. Better is 12.♘b3.

12...♖c8 13.♕g2

White should reject this move on principle, as it weakens the c3-knight.

13...♘ge5 14.0-0-0

White might have considered getting to castle queenside an accomplishment. The problem is that he's effectively down a full rook as it's currently buried on the h1 square.

14...♕a5 15.a3 ♘b4 16.♗d4

Can a2-a3 be the right move if it doesn't prevent ...♘c6-b4? On 16.axb4, we have 16...♕a1+ 17.♔d2 ♕xb2 18.♘e2 ♖xc2+ 19.♔e1 ♕xb4+ 20.♔f2 f5 21.exf5 ♖xf5, which is crushing for Black. Or 16.axb4 ♕a1+ 17.♔d2 ♕xb2 18.♘xe5 ♕xc3+ 19.♔e2 ♗xe5 20.♗e3 ♕xb4 21.♖c1 ♗b2 22.c3 ♕a4 23.♖d1 ♗xc3, and the king is covered by two pawns for fig leaves.

16...♖xc3! 17.♗xc3

White can't seem to catch a break: 17.axb4 ♕a1+ 18.♔d2 ♘xf3+ 19.♕xf3 ♖xf3 20.♖xa1 ♗xd4, winning for Black; or 17.bxc3 ♕xa3+ 18.♔d2 ♘xf3+ 19.♕xf3 ♗xd4 20.♗e2 ♗e5 21.cxb4 ♕xb4+ 22.♔e3 f5, winning.

17...♘a2+ 18.♔d2 ♘xc3 19.bxc3 ♗h6+ 20.♔e1 ♕xc3+ 21.♘d2 ♗xd2+ 22.♖xd2 ♘f3+ 23.♔d1 ♘xd2 0-1

White resigns, as he cannot play 24.♕xd2 since 24...♕f3+ picks up the h1-rook.

Game 20

Martín del Campo, Jorge (2465) – Verduga Zavala, Denis (2405)
[B76]
Santa Clara (Cuba) 1990

1.e4 c5 2.♘f3 d6 3.d4 cxd4 4.♘xd4 ♘f6 5.♘c3 g6 6.♗e3 ♗g7 7.f3 ♘c6 8.♕d2 0-0 9.g4 ♗xg4 10.fxg4 ♘xg4 11.♗g1 e6 12.h4 h5 13.♗e2 ♗h6

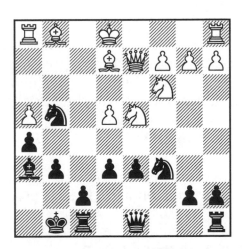

In Game 18, White exchanged knights and opened up the b-file for Black with 13.♘xc6 bxc6. After advancing his queen to d3, the resulting position allowed Black to anchor his knight on e5 with tempo: 14.♗e2 ♘h6 15.♕d3 ♘e5. However, on the plus side he only had one set of knights to deal with, so we shall see how the present game deviates and if it saves White's idea of ♗e3-g1.

14.♕d1 ♘ce5 15.♗xg4 ♘xg4

To challenge the g4-knight, White will have to maneuver one of his own knights to e3 or f2, or (later in the game) to e5. One of the pluses of the ♘d4xc6 plan as in Game 18 is that, with a pair of knights off the board, the simple ♗f1-e2 challenges the g4 square.

16.♕d3

All of your pieces should be involved in the game, so ♖h1-h3 is a logical move compared to moving the queen once again. If this move seems odd, look at the position and think about the other games where the king's rook never moved, with a bishop blocking g1. 16.♖h3 is a fairly natural move in the context of the overall position on the board. Normally, ♖h3 or ♖a3 in an opening is the mark of a total beginner, but everything in chess is based on the concrete position.

16...a6 17.♘b3 ♕e7

White has no natural plan for development, so he moves his knight out of the center in order to apply pressure with ♖a1-d1. The simple retreat to ♘f3 would seem to cover more active squares. Either way, White appears to be struggling for a constructive plan.

18.♖d1 ♖ad8 19.♗b6 ♖d7

White banks everything on disturbing Black's rook and queenside, but it's far from enough. Black's position is rock-solid with no weaknesses.

20.♔e2 ♘e5 21.♕d4 ♖c8 22.♘a5

White places his knight on the rim to deny Black the c4 square.

22...♘g4 23.♖h3 d5 24.♕a4?

After 22...d5, White should make a little move to control some squares like a2-a3. The text move is a blunder, however: White has gone into panic mode and hands the game to Black.

24...♕d6 25.♘xd5

Another blunder, but a solid defense is not to be found: 25.♗g1 b5 26.♕d4 b4 27.♕b6 ♕f8 28.♘a4 ♖xc2+ 29.♔e1 ♖dc7 30.♘b3 ♖7c6 31.♕b7 ♖6c4 32.♘ac5 ♖xb2, and White is overwhelmed by Black's forces.

25...exd5 0-1

Game 21

Burghardt, József (2160) – Pálkövi, József (2439) [B76]
Hungarian Team Chp 2011

1.e4 c5 2.♘f3 d6 3.d4 cxd4 4.♘xd4 ♘f6 5.♘c3 g6 6.♗e3 ♗g7 7.f3 0-0 8.♕d2 ♘c6 9.g4 ♗xg4 10.fxg4 ♘xg4 11.♘b3

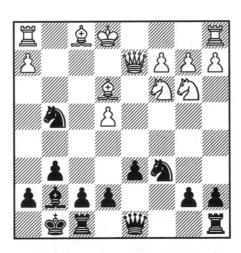

11.♘b3 has replaced 11.♗g1 as White's best try for advantage. While it is true with these lines that White is able to castle, it is far from an easy game and both sides have chances.

11...a5

This is the most popular move for Black, trying to provoke a2-a4 in reply. Worthy of consideration now is 12.♗b5.

12.a4 d5

What on the surface may appear to be a pawn blunder is actually a tactical resource to impede White's progress and make it difficult to castle queenside.

13.exd5 ♘xe3 14.♕xe3 ♗xc3+ 15.bxc3

On 15.♕xc3 ♕xd5 16.♖g1 ♘b4, White's king is stuck in the center.

15...♕xd5 16.♖g1 ♕d6

If Black is playing for a knockout punch, he might consider 16...♖ad8. Retreating the queen to d6 signals that he's just as happy to win an ending, as he eyes the h2-pawn.

17.♖g4 ♕xh2

Black gladly grabs the pawn, increasing the probability of winning the ending. For his part, White leaves the pawn undefended so that he can castle and get his queen rook into the game.

18.0-0-0 ♖ad8 19.♖e1 ♖d5

White's g5-rook and Black's d5-rook appear to only be guarding their respective a-pawns. Clearly not the case, but it's an interesting position.

20.♖e4 ♖fd8

Now the purpose of lifting the rooks is clear, and obviously it was not to guard the pawns on the wings.

21.♗d3

If shutting down the rooks is White's greatest concern, then 21.&d3 may be a reasonable move. If White wants to weaken e7, putting pressure on the knight, then 21.&b5 may be a better plan. Both moves have merit – it's a choice of how you want to approach the position.

21...&g7

Black takes time to lift his king to g7, not for any one specific reason but for a bunch of little ones. For example, the king guards h6; he now sits on a square of the opposite color to White's bishop; and he avoids back-rank tricks and prepares ...f7-f5 should he ever be ready to get that idea in.

22.&d2 &d6

Black's triple threat pins the bishop to the knight.

23.&c4 &c5

The pin is broken and Black makes it clear that he believes he can win the ending.

24.&e2 h5

Black's kingside is fairly well protected – at the very least, the h5 square is. Therefore, Black advances the pawn, making the transition to any endgame more problematic for White.

25.&g2

A minor error by White. Going to g2 first allows Black to kick the queen and to improve his rooks' deployment.

25...&g5 26.&h2 &d7 27.&f1 e6 28.&h4 &e7

Black is like an Olympic gymnast, keeping his core tight as the preliminary step before attempting any dangerous maneuvers.

29.&ef4 f5

The pawns are ready to roll and White's queen at h4 and rook at f4 are awkwardly placed.

30.♖4f2 ♖g4 31.♕h2 ♕h4

Black could begin the pawn roll with 30...e5, yet he seems intent on offering the queen trade to continue to push White back. Black is doing well; White's next move is fatal.

32.♖e1??

Trading queens with 32.♕xh4 was obligatory.

32...♖xc4 33.♗xc4 ♕xc4 34.♕g3?

White's chance to play on is 34.♖d2 ♖e7 35.♔b2 b5 36.axb5 ♕xb5+ 37.♔c1 ♕c4 38.♖d6 ♔f7 39.♕g3 ♕c5 40.♖g1 ♘e5 41.♖d4 ♘g4, but Black is still crushing.

34...♕a2 0-1

White must give up his queen with ♕d3 to stop ...♕a1#.

Chapter 5

9.♗c4 ♘xd4

Game 22

Vertesi, Jan – Teufel, Jürgen (2215) [B77]
Bavarian Chp, Krumbach 1981

1.e4 c5 2.♘f3 d6 3.d4 cxd4 4.♘xd4 ♘f6 5.♘c3 g6 6.♗e3
♗g7 7.f3 0-0 8.♕d2 ♘c6 9.♗c4 ♘xd4

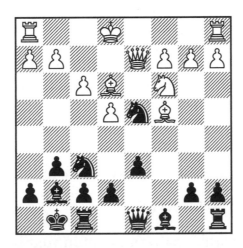

This game is different because previously we've only played
...♘c6xd4 when White fails to play ♗f1-c4. Now let's look at ideas
of challenging White's light-squared bishop right from the start.

10.♗xd4 ♗e6

Black immediately contests the c4 square, forcing White to make
the critical decision whether to retreat to b3 or to exchange at e6.
Had I suggested this move 10 years ago, many players would have
scoffed at playing an old and forgotten idea, yet American Super-
GM Hikaru Nakamura played this very line in 2012. Often in chess,
what is old will become new again, and players below professional
level should worry less about opening theory and more about pattern recognition and understanding openings.

11.♗b3 ♕a5

The ideas for Black have a very natural flow to them: one idea leads to the next.

12.0-0-0 ♗xb3

White could ease the pressure in this situation by castling king-side. One has to wonder if he is trapped in his own thematic under-standing of the position, unable to consider the simple question of which way to castle. Just because we've played one way 100 times before does not mean we should silence the inner voice that tells us to consider all options.

13.cxb3 ♖fc8 14.♔b1 ♖c6

If you have Black here, you have to feel good, even though the game is still virtually equal. At the very least, you are the one dictating the pace of the game.

15.h4 h5

Black correctly slows White down before resuming his own attack.

16.g4 ♖ac8 17.gxh5 ♕xh5

Here is an important pattern to put in your back pocket. There is no tax on the black queen for swinging to the kingside to snatch the pawn and defend; she can swing right back to the queenside. It takes White more time to get the attack started again than it does for the queen to swing back and forth.

18.♕f2

White guards the pawn and stays connected to the bishop in the most passive fashion possible. Far better is 18.♕d3.

18...b5 19.♖dg1 b4 20.♘e2? ♖c2

White's fate was sealed when he allowed Black to penetrate to the second rank. The old maxim, *"the best defense is a solid offense,"* might have led White to find 20.♖g5, forcing the black queen to h8. The rest of the game is a systematic thrashing.

21.♖c1 ♘xe4 22.fxe4 ♗xd4 23.♕xd4 ♕xe2 24.♖cg1 e5 0-1

Game 23

Hou Yifan (2606) – Cmilyte, Viktorija (2524) [B77]
Sportaccord blitz, Beijing 2012

1.e4 c5 2.♘c3 g6 3.♘f3 ♗g7 4.d4 cxd4 5.♘xd4 ♘c6 6.♗e3 d6 7.♗c4 ♘f6 8.f3 0-0 9.♕d2 ♘xd4 10.♗xd4 ♗e6 11.♗b3

White's move order is different from the previous game, but with 11.♗b3 we arrive at the same position.

11...♖c8

Black plays the old-school ...♖a8-c8 and turns it into a new-school attack.

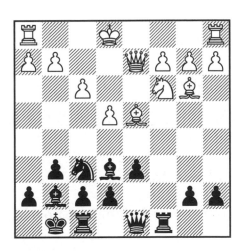

12.0-0-0 ♕a5 13.♔b1 ♖fd8

Here is another example with the idea of ...♖fd8. In the previous game, this move was almost an afterthought. This time it plays a key role in Black's victory.

14.♖he1 b5 15.♘d5 ♕xd2

Black is about equal here. In chess, Black must get equal before she can move ahead.

16.♖xd2 ♗xd5 17.exd5 ♖d7

After the trades, Black has two pawns to defend – e7 and a7; ...♖d8-d7 defends both neatly.

18.a4 a6

Often it's the simple moves that make a difference. Black holds the b5 square with ...a7-a6, which incidentally limits the scope of white's light-squared bishop. Chess is often made up of tens if not hundreds of these little battles that determine who wins the game. My theory is that you need to learn to "control and contain" before you can travel abroad and conquer.

19.c3 ♖b7

White fails to see the power of 19...♖b7, treating it as simply a developing move, and overlooks the dynamic threat that it poses.

20.axb5 axb5 21.♔c2

Pressuring e7 with 21.♖de2 would maintain the equilibrium by forcing Black to defend.

21...b4 22.♗a4 bxc3 23.♗xc3 ♘xd5

White didn't see this shot coming and now has a lost game.

24.♖xd5 ♖xb2+

If White now captures 25.♔xb2 ♗xc3+ 26.♔b3 ♗xe1, she is two pawns down with only a hope and a prayer that opposite-colored bishops will offer her some miraculous drawing chances.

25.♔d1

White makes the fatal mistake of assessing the position incorrectly. Keeping both sets of rooks and winning back the pawns, White falsely believes she has winning chances, when she should be fighting for the miracle draw with 25.♔xb2. This is a common affliction among many players: they can see ahead many moves and the resulting critical position, but it's their *assessment* of that position that leads to their demise.

25...♖xc3 26.♖xe7 ♗h6

Suddenly, breaking up the extra pawns comes at the price of a mating attack and the direct threat of ...♖c3-c1 with mate.

27.♔e1 ♖xg2 28.♖e2 ♖c1+ 29.♖d1 ♖g1+ 0-1

White ends up losing a piece with nothing to show for it, so she resigns.

Game 24

Ortiz Suárez, Isan Reynaldo (2612) – Gagare, Shardul (2419)
[B77]
Barberà del Vallès Open, Spain 2013

1.e4 c5 2.♘f3 d6 3.d4 cxd4 4.♘xd4 ♘f6 5.♘c3 g6 6.♗e3 ♗g7 7.f3 ♘c6 8.♕d2 0-0 9.♗c4 ♘xd4 10.♗xd4 ♗e6 11.♗b3 ♕a5 12.0-0-0 ♖fc8 13.♔b1 b5

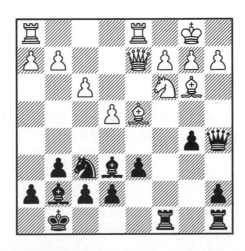

Chapter 5

When ...b7-b5 is uncontested, it's always an attractive option worthy of consideration. If White plays ♗xe6, the resulting pawn structure takes away the d5 square from the knight so Black should be feeling fairly confident here.

14.♖he1 ♗xb3 15.cxb3 ♖ab8

White having shifted his focus to the center with ♖he1, now the position is screaming for e4-e5, challenging Black's center and fighting for control of the a1-h8 diagonal. Black has his rook well placed, yet there is no apparent entry point to pry open the white king.

16.a3

White creates a target and is virtually begging Black to play ...b5-b4, creating an entry point for an attack. The simple 16.e5 would have kept the slight advantage that he appears to be giving away.

16...b4 17.♘a2 ♛b5 18.a4 ♛b7

With a casual look you might not see the weakness in this position; however, before 16.a3 White's queenside pawns were fairly solid. Now the b3-pawn is weak and, while it appears that Black's b4-pawn shields White's b3-pawn, it is weak nonetheless.

19.e5 ♘d5 20.exd6 ♘c3+

Black finds a way to reach the b3 square. Once you understand where the true weakness lies, the tactics are easier to find.

21.bxc3 bxc3 22.♛c2 ♛xb3+ 23.♛xb3 ♖xb3+ 24.♔c2 ♖b2+ 25.♔d3 ♖xa2

Black comes out of this with a nice position, yet White will retain a playable game if he simply plays 26.dxe7.

26.♖xe7??

Endings are a race to the finish line, so by capturing dxe7 White's pawn would be one square closer to queening. If you simply think

76

"race to the finish," it will guide your analysis in finding the best move. Had White played correctly, Black would have had to play ...♖c8-e8, slowing down his progress. The blunder 26.♖xe7 allows Black "time" and time is what the race to the finish is all about.

26...♗xd4 27.d7 ♖f8

When White looked ahead and saw this position in his mind's eye, I wonder if he believed he had 27.♔xd4 only to realize later that it loses after 27...♖d2+ 28.♖xd2 cxd2. If that is not true, then he believed that 27.d7 was winning and overlooked 27...♖f8 which holds the position.

28.♖e8 ♗f6

White is completely busted now − Black has multiple ways to finish him off.

29.♔e3 ♗d8 30.♔d3 ♖d2+ 31.♖xd2 cxd2 32.♔xd2 f5 33. ♔d3 ♔f7 34.♖e5 ♗c7 35.♖c5 ♗b6 0-1

Game 25

Hartman, Brian (2360) − Bailey, Doug (2355) [B77]
Toronto Open 1992

1.e4 c5 2.♘f3 d6 3.d4 cxd4 4.♘xd4 ♘f6 5.♘c3 g6 6.♗e3 ♗g7 7.f3 0-0 8.♕d2 ♘c6 9.♗c4 ♘xd4 10.♗xd4 ♗e6 11.♗b3 ♕d7

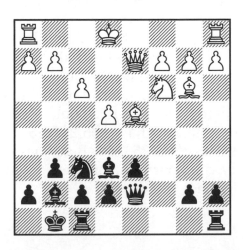

Chapter 5

A very unusual move! This first appeared as a novelty by GM Bent Larsen in Buenos Aires 1991. No doubt Bailey (playing Black) was influenced by Larsen's idea. The move connects the rooks, it supports the black bishop at e6, and it avoids the forced simplification lines that can occur after ...♕d8-a5 when White plays ♘c3-d5. At the very top levels, 11...♕d7 has appeared only a few times, garnering fairly solid results. It's worthy of consideration as another item for your toolbox.

12.h4 a5

Black boldly announces to White: "If it's a race you want, it's a race we shall have!"

13.a4 ♗xb3

If this were a game of chicken, White has lost, yielding the initiative. I don't like White's idea one bit – he's creating a weakness at b3 and, as we've already seen, this innocuous formation can mushroom into trouble. Castling queenside and leaving the pawn structure intact was a better option.

14.cxb3 ♕e6 15.h5 ♕xb3

White plans to lure the black queen into grabbing pawns, away from the defense of her king.

16.hxg6 fxg6 17.♘d5 ♘xd5 18.♗xg7 ♖f7!

The bishop is not poisoned, but it might be tainted. There are many complicated lines that go beyond the event horizon of a mortal chessplayer to determine the outcome, so Black seeks to clarify the position and stay in control of a winning game. Here is just one example of the craziness that could occur upon capturing: 18...♔xg7 19.♕h6+ ♔f6 20.♕h4+ ♔e5 21.♕g5+ ♔e6 22.♕g4+ ♖f5 23.exf5+ gxf5 24.♖h6+ ♘f6 25.♕d4. Black has compensation for the exchange and a good position, but there are many other checks and lines that might not end as well.

19.♖xh7 ♕e3+

Black can neither capture the rook as it leads to mate, nor play 19...♖xg7 as it allows White to escape into an equal ending. The text move maintains Black's winning advantage.

20.♕xe3 ♘xe3 21.♖h8+ ♔xg7 22.♖xa8 ♘c2+ 23.♔d2 ♘xa1

The combination ends and White takes inventory to discover that he is now completely lost. A great lesson here is not to play recaptures automatically and to think every move out; only by doing so did Black find 18...♖f7.

24.♔c3 ♖f8 25.♖xa5 ♖c8+ 26.♔d3 ♘c2 27.♖a7 ♖c7 28.g3 ♘b4+ 29.♔e3 ♘c6 30.♖a8 ♘e5 0-1

In summary, 9...♘xd4, followed by ...♗c8-e6, provides Black a valid option even if White is trying to steer for the main-line Dragon with 9.♗c4.

Now let's add another alternative to widen our understanding.

9.0-0-0 d5

Game 26

Voitsikh, A. – Rusinkevich, Nina [B76]
USSR Jr. Team Chp, Riga 1954

　1.e4 c5 2.♘f3 d6 3.d4 cxd4 4.♘xd4 ♘f6 5.♘c3 g6 6.♗e3 ♗g7 7.f3 ♘c6 8.♕d2 0-0 9.0-0-0

This is a position we've visited many times before. By now, I hope you are open to the idea that chess begins on move 1 and not on move 23!

　9...d5

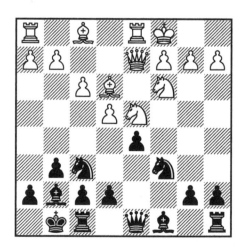

Yet another way for Black to mix it up with White and drag her down a rabbit hole. Obviously we don't want to hand White a pawn, so we will never use this move if White plays 9.♗c4.

Statistically, Black has scored better with 9...d5 than with 9...♘xd4, but both are solid options. You might be surprised to learn that when White fails to play 9.♗c4 and Black continues with 9...♗d7, Black scores poorly compared to 9...d5 or 9...♘xd4.

10.♘xc6 bxc6

The most popular move is 10.exd5, favored by the likes of Kasparov and Anand. Known proponents of 10.♘xc6 are Timman and Sokolov. My experience with the casual class player is that they like 10.♘xc6, so it's wise to become well acquainted with the patterns in this line.

11.exd5 ♛a5

Black prefers to activate her pieces to trifling with silly pawns. Of course, I'm joking. We'll see later on how the dynamic 11...cxd5 leads to intense warfare.

12.dxc6

If White plays 12.♗c4, Black should pin the pawn to the queen with 12...♖d8. As played in this game, activating the bishop is a fine idea. I always prefer a straightforward concept that is easy to remember and contributes to fundamental development, as opposed to understanding theoretical opening lines.

12...♗e6 13.a3 ♖fd8

Had White been reading this book, she may have favored 13.♔b1, as it frees the c3-knight to move without Black's being able to trade queens with check. I point this out again, as you need to be hyper-aware of this pattern to avoid the trick where White moves the knight and takes the e7-pawn with check. If you need a refresher, please go over Game 7 again.

14.♛e2 ♖xd1+

White is blocking in her bishop, but this is actually fine. The idea here is to exchange off a set of rooks, but it also allows White the possibility of streaming her queen out to b4 and asking Black if she wants to trade queens.

15.♕xd1 ♖d8

My objection to recapturing with the queen is based on my belief that White's plan was to have ♕e2-b5 at her disposal. If you're not willing to play ♘xd1 because it may weaken your castled king, then don't play 14.♕e2.

16.♕e2 ♘d5

White has proven my point; her position is almost identical to what it was after 14.♕e2 but she's allowed Black to improve her position.

17.♘xd5 ♕xd5 18.c7 ♗xb2+

Pushing the c-pawn leads to forced mate. However, even without this foolish move White's situation is grim. After 18.♕d2 ♗xb2+ 19.♔d1 ♕a5 20.♗d3 ♗c3 21.♕c1 ♗d5, Black is still dictating the pace of White's demise.

19.♔xb2 ♕a2+ 0-1

Mate next move is unstoppable.

Game 27

Byvshev, Vasily – Beilin, Mikhail [B76]
USSR Chp, Leningrad 1955

1.e4 c5 2.♘f3 d6 3.d4 cxd4 4.♘xd4 ♘f6 5.♘c3 g6 6.♗e3 ♗g7 7.f3 ♘c6 8.♕d2 0-0 9.0-0-0 d5 10.♘xc6 bxc6 11.exd5 ♘xd5

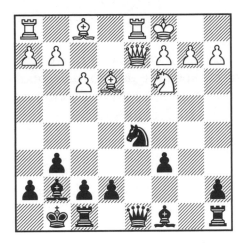

In the previous game, after White played 11.exd5, Black activated the queen with 11...♕a5, hoping to put pressure on the white king. This time we'll look at capturing the d5-pawn with the knight, increasing the scope of Black's Dragon bishop.

12.♘xd5 cxd5 13.♕xd5 ♕c7

If Black did not have this tricky line, he would simply be a pawn down with little to show for it. Let's call this pattern "the hanging-rook line." Historically, White has done very poorly when capturing the rook. Doing so requires accurate play to achieve equality. Play could proceed along these lines: 14.♕xa8 ♗f5 15.♕xf8+ ♔xf8 16.♖d2 ♕b8 17.b3 e6 18.♗c4 ♕e5 19.♗d4 ♕a5 20.♗xg7+ ♔xg7 21.♖e2 ♕xa2 22.♖d1, and White is equal.

14.♕c5 ♕b7

White sidesteps the forcing lines that occur with the rook capture. Instead, White offers a queen trade, which Black refuses. Take note of this position with the opposing queens, as it's a common theme. Often you'll see a player trying to defuse the tension in a position and offer an exchange over and over to decrease the amount of firepower on the board.

15.c3

White must decide between the text move and 15.♕a3. In theory, I prefer 15.♕a3, as it keeps the pawn shield on its original squares and therefore at its strongest, and it also moves the queen out of the way before Black's rook comes to c8.

15...♗f5 16.♕b5 ♕c7

White again offers the exchange of queens, which Black wisely declines.

17.♕c4 ♕e5

It's getting old, right? In a strange way, these little dances remind me of a king-and-pawn ending where the kings are battling for the opposition. King-and-pawn endings can be very tricky. Here, just remember that if you have the positionally stronger side, you should avoid the exchange.

18.♗d2?

White has to play 18.♗f4, pushing the queen back and taking away the b8 square from the rook. The text move boxes White in and weakens his position.

18...♖fd8 19.f4 ♕a5 20.♗e2??

It's absolute madness to forget the queen dance, for here 20.♕a6! is best.

20...♖ac8 21.♕a6 ♗xc3 0-1

White rightly resigns, as mate is unstoppable. At first glance you might believe that 22.♕xa5 slows Black down, but the conclusion is immediate after 22...♗xd2!.

Game 28

Zhilin, Vitaly – Gufeld, Eduard [B76]
USSR Chp, Novosibirsk 1962

1.e4 c5 2.♘f3 d6 3.d4 cxd4 4.♘xd4 ♘f6 5.♘c3 g6 6.♗e3 ♗g7 7.f3 0-0 8.♕d2 ♘c6 9.0-0-0 d5 10.♘xc6 bxc6 11.exd5 ♘xd5 12.♗d4

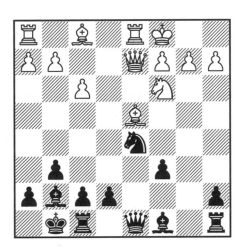

Whereas in Game 27 White tried 12.♘xd5, here White offers the bishop trade. I was careful to choose this game not so much because of our 9...d5 theme, but to illustrate why pattern recognition is important.

12...e5 13.♗c5 ♗e6

Black offers the exchange in order to gain quick development for his pieces and to lock down the center.

14.♗xf8 ♕xf8 15.♗c4 ♗h6 0-1

Did you see it coming? Where did we see that move before? In Game 8, where 9...♘xd4 was played, we also had the shot of an undefended ...♗g7-h6 where capturing would have allowed a mate at c2. In the present game, Black wins the queen because the bishop is supported by the queen from f8.

Game 29

Sorri, Kari Juhani – Arnaudov, Petar [B76]
World U26 Team Chp, Harrachov 1967

The theme I wish to introduce in this game is that your opponent's threat to win an exchange doesn't always need to be defended. It takes time for the minor piece to attack and capture a rook; in return, the side that gives up the exchange often gains an initial burst of energy. If you can get your head around this "energy" concept instead of thinking in traditional chess terms, it is easier to conceptualize that this short-term initiative (energy) is something that must be used before it dissipates. It's like having the momentum in sports: you need to ride that advantage as long as it lasts, and with the loss of the exchange you often gain momentum. So in the following game a rook is attacked at f8 and the best course is not to attempt to defend it – just let it happen, and in the case of this game, we quickly get to build a solid center.

1.e4 c5 2.♘f3 ♘c6 3.d4 cxd4 4.♘xd4 g6 5.♘c3 ♗g7 6.♗e3 ♘f6 7.f3 d6 8.♕d2 0-0 9.h4

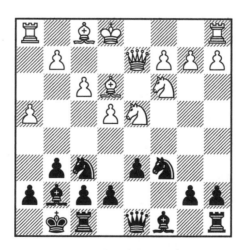

As you are well aware by now, the objective in this book is to help you increase your ability to recognize patterns in chess. I would be woefully deficient in my task if we did not pause here to call out this pattern of the pawn storm. It's a tricky one and it's often overlooked as a pattern because of its ubiquitous nature. It will appear when you play White with little concern whether your first move is e4 or d4. If you have the misfortune of having the black pieces, the pawn-storm pattern won't hesitate for a moment to test the competence and cohesiveness of your men. It gallops onward like the fifth Horseman of the Apocalypse, yet for all its bravado it has no special power to harm you and only becomes a cause for concern if you don't recognize it for what it is and come to fear the pawn attack on the flank. It is a natural reaction for amateur players to have an emotional response to a mass of pawns rolling toward their king.

Let's strip away the emotion and take an objective look at what's going on. First of all, if chess were as simple as running the flank pawns up the board and winning, there would be no books about endgames, and draws would be a fairly rare event. So if defeat is not immediate, what's going on? Well, from the aggressor's perspective, either he's playing known opening lines (or thinks he is), or else he's a caveman. From your side of the board, if you are made anxious by this attack (and there is no shame in admitting it), as many players are, then take a few deep silent breaths and even take a minute to get a sip of water before you move on. It is better to pull your emotions back under control than to get into a slugging match with a fool, or – even worse – to attempt a slugging match with someone who has studied the lines. A general rule is that a premature attack on the flank is best thwarted by a counter in the center. Don't focus excessively on the attack to the exclusion of the center: and even if it's a well-known line, the center attack often keeps the game in equilibrium. So, relax and know that you are fine.

9...d5

Black takes the central counter approach and lets White know he's not worried about the pawn storm.

10.♘xc6 bxc6 11.0-0-0 ♗e6

Black's last move is a bit unorthodox. The normal 11...♕c7 steers back toward the patterns and formations we've seen in our other games. Astute readers will notice that Black played 9...d5 in response to 9.h4, and that's OK because the transposition idea has led us back to positions that could be reached by 9.0-0-0. You must be on the alert not to allow a transposition to get you on the wrong side of a bad position.

12.e5?

White makes a strategic mistake by not exchanging in the center with the idea of releasing the tension. White drives the knight to a strong square and secures the future of the d5-pawn.

12...♘d7 13.♗h6?

Did White believe that Black would exchange bishops, providing him a ready-made attack? Better was 13.f4, which gives up notions of immediate attacks in return for contesting the center.

13...♗xe5!

Black offers the minor exchange for the sake of building a formidable center. White can no longer afford second-best moves; he's made too many concessions.

14.♗xf8 ♕xf8

Note that if our bishop returns to g7, we have the potential for creating the pattern with ...♗h6 supported by the queen.

15.f4 ♗f6 16.g3 ♖b8

White slows down the flank attack and looks to consolidate his material edge into a playable middlegame. Black deploys his whole army to the queenside behind his strong pawn center.

17.♗h3?

White is drifting again. He's trading off Black's weakest piece with a piece that could participate in the game. What purpose will the rooks serve as Black pries apart the queenside? White needs to play the counterintuitive 17.b3 to slow Black down.

17...♗xh3 18.♖xh3 e6

White's position is hopeless, as Black will bring all of his pieces into the game supported by his curtain of pawns. White has an overworked knight plus two rooks that all told are worth about 13 points on the standard piece-value point scale.

We arrive at that figure by the standard values given in instructional books for novices, where the queen has a value of 9 points, a rook is worth 5, and a bishop and knight are worth 3 each. That's great advice for a beginner, but what about the advancing player – is there something more? Edward Lasker recognized this need for a different approach when he wrote, "It is difficult to compare the relative value of different pieces, as so much depends on the peculiarities of the position." Over the years, I've developed my own theory that provides a framework for analyzing a position and allows the player to work out a sense of the shifting value of the pieces in order to develop a deeper sense of the game. I've labeled this "the Theory of Diminishing and Increasing Values."

According to this theory, in the opening the queen is worth 6.5 points; as the games goes on and approaches an ending, or pieces and pawns are exchanged or moved in order to increase her mobility, her value may soar to as high as 12.

The knights early on in the opening are worth 3.75 points each and decrease in value as more pieces are developed. However, in a closed endgame they are worth 4, while in an open ending they might be worth only 2.5 whereas a bishop in that same position would be worth 4.2.

A pawn early on is worth only 1 point, a value which remains fixed for most the of game; however, in the ending a pawn racing to promotion may well end up being worth 3.5.

If a piece is overworked or out of play, we may in a given position saddle that piece with a value of 1 or even zero.

While my theory is not a complete system and it requires the student to come up with his own evaluations, it is a useful tool to help develop the sense that, during a game, the pieces increase and decrease in value as the position changes.

Let's go back to our two rooks and knight: one of the rooks is completely out of play and the knight is tied to c3 and can't move. Based on this position, right now on this move I assign a total value of 6 points to those three pieces.

19.a3

White should give up on the queenside and play 19.g4, praying to the gods that Black falters. Using our above assessment of 6 points makes this move easier to find as it activates the rook, increasing its value.

If White feels morally obligated to defend this hopeless position, I prefer 19.b3 and let Black find his win after 19...♛a3+.

19...♘b6 20.♛d3 ♘c4 21.b4 ♖xb4

Black must have been bewitched by the fact that White can recapture. Equally strong was the simple 21...a5.

22.axb4 ♛xb4 23.♖d2 ♝xc3 24.♖f2   0-1

White resigned rather than face 24...♛a3+ 25.♔d1 ♘b2+, winning the queen.

Game 30

Ljubojević, Ljubomir – Svensson, Gert [B76]
Zürich U20 1970

1.e4 c5 2.♘f3 d6 3.d4 cxd4 4.♘xd4 ♘f6 5.♘c3 g6 6.♝e3 ♝g7 7.f3 0-0 8.♛d2 ♘c6 9.0-0-0 d5 10.exd5 ♘xd5 11.♘xc6 bxc6 12.♝d4 e5

This pattern appears in many Dragon lines. White will offer the exchange of bishops by playing ♝e3-d4, and if Black wants active counterplay, he is almost always correct in playing ...e7-e5. Only if you can find an immediate refutation to ...e7-e5 or a much stronger move should you avoid it as Black.

13.♗c5 ♗e6 14.♗c4

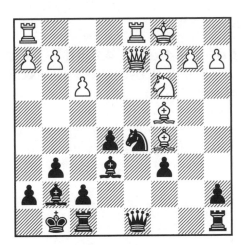

Game 13 saw 14.♗xf8 ♕xf8, and White lost his queen to the ...♗g7-h6 pattern. Here, White tries to keep the tension on the board.

14...♘xc3 15.♗xe6?

It is hard to imagine that a great GM like Ljubojević could overlook these tactics near the peak of his career. The clear path to safety is 15.♕xc3 ♕g5+ 16.♗e3 ♕xg2 17.♗xe6 fxe6 18.♕xc6 ♖ac8 19.♕xe6+, when both sides have equal chances.

15...♘xd1

White is now lost. All roads lead to ruin.

16.♗d7

16.♗xf8 ♕xf8 17.♕xd1 fxe6 would fare only slightly better than the text move.

16...♘xb2 17.♔xb2 ♖b8+ 18.♔c1 ♖b7 0-1

If the light-squared bishop withdraws from d7, Black has ...♖b1+ winning the queen. 19.♖d1 ♕b8 20.♕d3 ♖d8 brings the game to an end.

Game 31

Polgár, István (2370) – Dely, Péter (2480) [B76]
Toth Memorial, Kecskemét 1972

1.e4 c5 2.♘f3 d6 3.d4 cxd4 4.♘xd4 ♘f6 5.♘c3 g6 6.♗e3 ♗g7 7.f3 ♘c6 8.♕d2 0-0 9.0-0-0 d5 10.exd5 ♘xd5 11.♘xc6 bxc6 12.♗d4 e5 13.♗c5 ♗e6

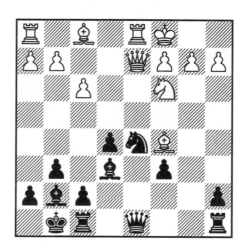

We have seen the foolhardy 14.♗c4 and we've seen 14.♗xf8. White has a third choice:

14.♘xd5 cxd5

White goes for the logical plan of exchanging knights in the center. Seems reasonable, given that Black's source of power in the Dragon often comes from the minor pieces. The downside to this is that Black now has a fortress of center pawns.

15.♗b5

White plays ♗f1-b5 in order to stop Black from saving the minor exchange with ...♖fe8. Set chess aside for a moment and look at this position as if it were a logic problem. Your friend has offered you candy, but you don't accept the offer right away. Now he sets the candy bowl on the coffee table and continues the conversation. Should you be concerned that he might suddenly jump up and return the bowl to the kitchen? Would you take time to position yourself to block his path to the kitchen? I hope you agree that that would be complete foolishness. What White has done by playing 15.♗b5 is far worse. Not only has he rejected the first offer of candy, he has now allowed Black to decide if White must eat chocolate or vanilla candy!

Did you figure out my obtuse little riddle? If Black wants to remove White's light-squared bishop, he plays ...♖fe8. If Black wants to remove White's dark-squared bishop, he leaves the rook on f8. If you're wondering why he doesn't take the rook, I can only say that it's simply what happened and White is a foolish man for lining his bishops up on the fifth rank.

15...d4

Black decides that White shall eat the chocolate candy.

16.♗xf8 ♕xf8 17.♔b1!

We jokingly give White an exclamation mark for learning the patterns taught in this book.

17...♖b8 18.♗a4 d3

Black correctly decides to dismantle his enormous pawn center. White is obligated to accept, and he must do so with extreme care!

19.cxd3 e4 20.d4 exf3

Both sides understand the dance, and find the correct moves.

21.gxf3??

Understandably, White underestimated the danger in the position. He needed to find 21.♖he1 fxg2 22.♕xg2 ♕b4 23.♖xe6 fxe6 24.♗b3 in order to stay in the game.

21...♕a3!

There are moves that are so powerful, the opponent can quickly lose the will to fight once the gravity of the situation is understood.

22.♗b3 ♖xb3 0-1

Resigning here is correct, as all roads lead swiftly to defeat:

a) 23.axb3 ♗f5+ 24.♕d3 ♕xb3 25.♕xf5 gxf5 26.♖hg1 ♔f8 wins;
b) 23.♖he1 ♖b8 24.♖xe6 fxe6 25.b3 ♕d6 wins.

Game 32

Hadjittofis, Yianakis – Whiteley, Andrew J. (2310) [B76]
Skopje Olympiad 1972

This game is similar to Game 27 in that we have the "opposing queens" pattern.

1.e4 c5 2.♘f3 d6 3.d4 cxd4 4.♘xd4 ♘f6 5.♘c3 g6 6.♗e3 ♗g7 7.f3 0-0 8.♕d2 ♘c6 9.0-0-0 d5 10.exd5 ♘xd5 11.♘xd5 ♕xd5 12.♘b3 ♕e5 13.♗d4 ♘xd4 14.♕xd4

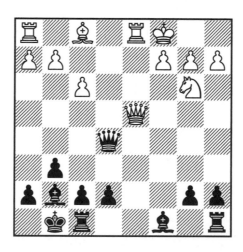

White offers the queen trade and we reach the first of our opposing-queen positions.

14...♕c7 15.♕c4

In Game 27, White played 14.♕c5 where the queen was supported by the dark-squared bishop on e3. This time, the queen uses the c4 square supported by the light-squared bishop on its home square. We can correctly assume this to be less dynamic, as the queen has not crossed the center line and the supporting piece, as mentioned, is undeveloped. Astute readers may have noticed that White could play 15.♕c5 supported by the b3-knight. However, this feels esthetically wrong and White may be tempting fate, as Black could try to punish him with ...♕f4+ followed by a sneaky move to f5 by the c8-bishop and a rook to the vacated square, i.e. 15...♕f4+ 16.♔b1 ♗f5 threatening ...♖f(a)c8.

15...♕b6 16.♗d3

White has developed his bishop awkwardly. Notice how developing the bishop has made the white queen less effective: she has fewer useful squares and is just waiting to be smacked around.

16...♕f6

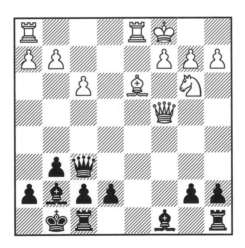

This is a great position for a discussion of king safety and attacking the king. The king is safest behind the formation of all three pawns on their original squares. Most players learn this as beginners, when they read and study a classic chess primer like Capablanca's *Chess Fundamentals*. Yet most players do not internalize the concept in a way that truly influences how they play the game. We fall in love with our favorite chess opening and play a move like ...h7-h6 to allow a bishop to retreat, or – as in the subject of this book – we have no Dragon without ...g7-g6 and ...♗f8-g7. These moves may be fine based on chess theory, or it may very well be that playing ...h7-h6 to enable the bishop to retreat was the best move on the board. All of that can be true while at the same time contradicting the principle that the strongest placement for the pawns is on their original squares, protecting the king like the guards at Buckingham Palace. Therefore, the power of 16...♕f6 is not that it threatens mate at b2. While that is a lofty goal, the power of ...♕b6-f6 is that the only defending move at White's disposal is 17.c3, and that displacement from the original square constitutes a weakness. That's the switch that needs to go on in your head for you to become a strong player. It's not that you are playing 16...♕f6 to threaten mate, but that you are playing it to provoke a weakness in White's position.

That is what attacking the king is all about: creating a weakness and then prying open the pawns to extract the king like a lobster tail from its shell.

17.c3 ♗e6 18.♕e4?

White's queen would be more effective on the second rank, and should seek shelter with 18.♕c5-f2. White's idea for getting her back to safety is as strange as ♗f1-d3 was.

18...♖fc8 19.♕e1

Why is e1 better than e2!? Black's next move threatens to strip the white king of his pawn cover. All because 16...♕f6 provoked the weakening c2-c3.

19...b5 20.♔b1 b4 21.♖c1 a5 22.♕d2

White's position is already compromised and moving the queen again will sink him further.

22...a4

As a general pattern, pawn storms done in pairs open more doors than a single pawn, White pushes h2-h4, and Black tosses a queenside pawn forward. White advances h4-h5 (or g2-g4) and Black gets another pawn move. In this game, White is not keeping up his share of the bargain, so Black is totally justified in running with two pawns.

23.♘d4 bxc3 24.bxc3 ♖ab8+   0-1

If White hides in the corner, he is mated with 25.♔a1 ♕xd4 26.cxd4 ♗xd4+ 27.♖c3 ♖xc3 28.♕b2 ♖c2 29.♖b1 ♖bxb2 30.♖xb2 ♖xb2 31.♗f1 ♖b4#.

25.♔c2 drops a piece to 25...♕xd4. Other moves that avoid mate are worse, like 25.♗b5 ♗f5+ 26.♔a1 ♖xc3 27.♖xc3 ♕xd4 28.♕xd4 ♗xd4 29.♔b2 ♖xb5+ 30.♔a3 ♗xc3, when White is down two bishops and can only delay mate by playing giveaway chess.

Chapter 7

//

9...a5

Game 33

Hloušek, Zdeněk – Kølbæk, Jens [B77]
World U26 Team Chp, Dresden 1969

    1.e4 c5 2.♘f3 d6 3.d4 cxd4 4.♘xd4 ♘f6 5.♘c3 g6 6.♗e3 ♗g7 7.f3 0-0 8.♗c4 ♘c6 9.♕d2 a5

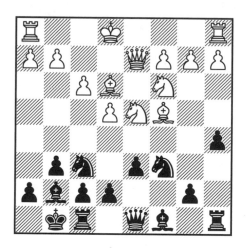

    Have you ever had that jolting feeling when a move sneaks up on you totally unexpectedly? Maybe you've had that feeling when you failed to see the original intent of a move and the plan doesn't become clear for several moves. Suddenly you see that piece taller, stronger, and more threatening as you realize what your opponent's been up to. This can easily happen with 9...a5, a move that has sneak-attack power!

    White has numerous options in dealing with 9...a5. In keeping with our focus on patterns, we can place all the moves into two groups – those that ignore ...a7-a5 and those that react to it and anticipate Black's intentions. Reactive moves include 10.a4, 10.0-0, 10.a3, and 10.♗b3. Moves that ignore it are 10.h4, 10.0-0-0, and

10.g4. For this first game, let's see what happens when White turns the proverbial blind eye to Black's designs.

10.h4 ♘e5

Black attacks the bishop and now White must retreat to e2. Unfortunately, he's about to find out why e2 is the only safe square. This game is an example of what happens when White plays thematic Dragon ideas without regard to the specifics of the position.

11.♗b3?

White can play 11.♗e2 or 11.♗b5, but he cannot play 11.♗b3 with impunity. A very useful trap to keep in mind, as by instinct a weaker player is going to be drawn to play ♗c4-b3.

11...a4

Take a moment and see if you can find the follow-up, but no worries if you can't, as it's not a "natural" idea.

12.♘xa4

Who thinks in the opening, right? White assumes Black is sacrificing a pawn to open up lines.

12...♖xa4 13.♗xa4 ♘c4

Black draws the bishop to the vulnerable a4 square so that he can drop the knight on c4, deflecting the queen from d2 to leave the a4-bishop hanging after ...♕d8-a5+. Ingenious, yet transparent – right? I feel for White. That jolting feeling must have hit him hard.

14.♕c3

It does not matter if White plays 14.♕e2, 14.♕d3, or the text 14.♕c3 – on all moves, Black is capturing the knight, which after a recapture leads to 15.♕xe3 ♕a5+ 16.♔f2 ♕xa4 and Black has two bishops against a rook. My general rule is that knight and bishop beat a rook, while two bishops mug a rook and take his wallet.

14...♘xe3 15.♔f2

White avoids the ...♕a5+ trap and hopes to recapture the knight with his king. Natural lines such as 15.♕xe3 ♕a5+ 16.c3 ♕xa4 17.g4 h5 lead to a clearly winning position for Black; proper play and the minor pieces should do serious damage to the rook. With that assessment, if White was considering resigning, I can respect his attempt, with 15.♔f2, to mix it up.

15...♘eg4+

Capturing the knight meets with an immediate king-and-queen fork when the other knight takes the e4-pawn. With the queen knight at e5 and the king knight at f6, together they control an interesting pattern of squares in c4, g4, and e4, with f3 occasionally coming into play. One knight rips the center open and the other one often delivers the crushing blow.

This pattern should be the only proof required to demonstrate that Black's 11...a4 and 12...♖xa4 are powerful moves, and that the theme of 9...a5 is not to be ignored.

16.♔e2 ♕b6

Complete domination by the black knights. Black need not retreat the g4-knight; by applying pressure to d4 instead, he can answer 17.fxg4 with 17...♘xe4, which hits the queen and discovers the g7-bishop's attack on the d4-knight. For double extra chocolate sauce, 17...♘xe4 permits ...♗xg4+ too, or (if you prefer) White's goose is cooked.

17.♖ad1

The best defensive move is not enough.

17...e5 18.fxg4 exd4 19.♕xd4 ♗xg4+ 20.♔f2 0-1

White blunders in a lost position and resigns immediately in view of 20...♘xe4+ 21.♔e3 ♗xd4+, winning White's queen. However, Black also wins on 20.♔e1 ♕a5+ 21.c3 ♗xd1; alternatively, he can try to move in for the kill with 21...b5 22.♗c2 ♛xa2 23.♖d2 ♖e8 24.♛xd6 ♛a1+ 25.♗d1 ♞xe4 with a crushing position.

Game 34

Frilling, Frank – Watson, John L. [B77]
U.S. Open 1969

IM John Watson manipulates the black pieces like a magician making doves appear out of nowhere. If you are not familiar with IM Watson, I highly recommend his book *Secrets of Modern Chess Strategy: Advances since Nimzowitsch,* published in 1999. Players from beginner to master and beyond can learn something from this book. It's worth reading at least twice; it's really that good.

1.e4 c5 2.♞f3 d6 3.d4 cxd4 4.♞xd4 ♞f6 5.♞c3 g6 6.♗e3 ♗g7 7.f3 0-0 8.♛d2 ♞c6 9.♗c4 a5 10.♗b3

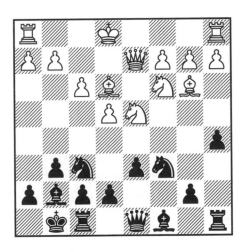

We can put White's move into the reactive ideas of how to deal with ...a7-a5, yet ♗c4-b3 is such a normal move in many Dragon lines. Maybe he has not fully accounted for the dangers of Black's pawn push.

10...♗d7 11.a3 a4 12.♗a2 ♛a5

White has taken a precautionary approach to dealing with ...a7-a5, avoiding the complete collapse that we saw in Game 28.

13.h4 ♖fc8 14.♘de2 ♘e5

The knight eyes c4, while the d7-bishop can aid in the potential advance of the b-pawn to b5. That's about all I would need to see to avoid castling long. As White, I would castle short here. Let the position and pawn structure be your guide. Take an overview of the strategic theme and don't worry about clairvoyance or calculating nine moves ahead.

15.0-0-0 ♗e6

White disagrees with my assessment and willingly goes into the line of fire. Perhaps he rejected castling short because of the liability of the h4-pawn. Pause and take a good hard look at this position: get a cup of coffee and take your time – you'll be amazed at the story that unfolds.

16.♘d5

White should not seek complications and instead should try to consolidate by exchanging bishops at e6 or by playing ♔b1. Creating complications when Black has his pieces fairly well aimed at your king is generally not a good idea.

16...♘xd5 17.♕xa5 ♘xe3

White captures the queen and Black smirks. "Whatever!" I can imagine that White is now in shock, and rightly so! There is no clear path to salvation for White, and if there were it would be difficult to recover psychologically after a blow such as this one. I can only imagine that he sat here for a very long time, realizing he was completely lost.

18.♕b6

All roads lead to ruin: 18.♕d2 ♗xa2 19.♕xe3 ♘c4 20.♕d4 ♖c6 21.♕xg7+ ♔xg7 22.♘c3 ♘xa3 23.bxa3 ♖xc3 24.♔b2 ♖ac8 25.♔xa2 ♖xc2+ 26.♔b1 ♖xg2, and Black wins easily.

18...♖xc2+ 19.♔b1 ♗xa2+ 20.♔xa2 ♘xd1 21.♖xd1 ♘c4 22. ♕c7 ♖xb2+ 23.♔a1 ♖xe2+ 24.♔b1 ♘xa3+ 25.♔c1 ♗b2# 0-1

A wonderful queen sacrifice, and Black checkmates with an unusual final position.

Game 35

Efimov, Igor (2405) – Zilberstein, David (2235) [B77]
Hradec Králové 1988

1.e4 c5 2.♘f3 d6 3.d4 cxd4 4.♘xd4 ♘f6 5.♘c3 g6 6.♗e3 ♗g7 7.f3 0-0 8.♗c4 ♘c6 9.♕d2 a5 10.♗b3 ♘e5

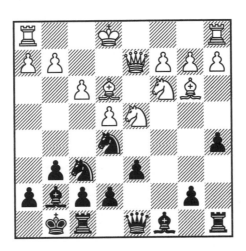

In our previous game, IM Watson played 10...♗d7, supporting the ...b7-b5 push, whereas in this game Black plays 10...♘e5. White should recognize the common pattern of Black's striving to get his knight to c4 to break the connection between the dark-squared bishop and the queen.

11.h4

White fails to recognize that the texture of the game has changed and plays as if Black has trotted out a main-line Dragon. Available options for White are to castle short or to play a2-a4 to stop the black a-pawn's advance. If you find yourself in a position where you are unsure of the correct way to proceed, it is better to play a solid prophylactic move than to try to force your way back to main-line theory, which may very well no longer apply.

11...a4 12.♗xa4 ♘c4

Black's pawn thrust has displaced the bishop and quickly yields him the coveted c4 square, with a clear advantage.

13.♕e2 d5!

There is no way for White to exploit this move – he is in immediate trouble.

Playing ...d6-d5 to break White's grip on the center is a common theme. Taking the e3-bishop would quickly release the tension and allow White to escape. A good chess maxim is, "The threat is stronger than the execution," and it applies in this very position, as taking the bishop would be very weak. The maxim is often attributed to Nimzowitsch regarding a famous smoking story; in fact, though, the expression had been around before Nimzowitsch was ever born. Famous chess historian Edward Winter has published on his chesshistory.com Web site that it was first formulated by the Austrian master Karl Eisenbach (1836-1894).

14.e5 ♘h5

White is completely overwhelmed: Black is threatening a fork at g3, the pawn at e5 is hanging, and Black can still chop off the bishop at e3.

15.♖g1

We've all heard the expression that "time is money," but, in chess, time is also a currency to be traded. Moving the rook to safety takes time that White can't afford to spend. In the larger scheme of things, which piece is more powerful, the black knight or the white rook? The black knight, of course! So a logical move would be to castle long and try to limit the damage.

15...♗xe5 16.g4 ♘xe3 17.♕xe3 ♗f4

White must decide between taking on a passive role for his queen with 18.♕f2, supporting the weak g3 square; or 18.♕d3, controlling more squares but allowing Black to knock him around on the kingside.

18.♕d3 ♗h2

Black has many promising tactical options. Everywhere he turns, he is sure to find a winning line: 18...e5 19.♘de2 d4 20.♘e4 ♕a5+ 21.c3 ♗e3.

19.♖h1 ♗g3+ 20.♔f1 ♘f4 21.♕d2 e5

This clearly looks less promising than playing ...e7-e5 on move 18. Taking inventory of the position, what did Black accomplish? White's rook was useless on g1, and by forcing White to play ♖h1, he needs to be careful so as not to allow White to slip back into the game.

22.♘de2 ♘xe2 23.♘xe2 ♗xh4

If the World Champion tells me that 22...♗xh4 is a sound move, I'm still not playing it. The best move is only one link in the chain, and I prefer not to have my links expose my king to a semi-open h-file. Therefore, I would play 23...♖xa4 to keep control of the game, when play could continue 24.♘xg3 ♕f6 25.♔g2 e4 26.fxe4 dxe4 27.♕e2 ♕xb2 and Black is doing very well.

24.♕h6

Why rush into the attack and leave the bishop hanging? 24.♗b3 would create an immediate threat by attacking the d4-pawn. If I can save a hanging piece by bringing it to the aid of my attack, why would I not do so?

24...g5 25.♘g3

White may want to consider 25.♗b5.

25...♖a6 0-1

White can save his queen (for now) with 26.♕h5. However, that was his swindle square for this knight. After 26...♖xa4, the rook can swing back to a6 and prevent the queen from creating counterplay.

Game 36

Pletánek, Jan (2236) – Jirovský, Miloš (2450) [B77]
Czech Chp 2002

1.e4 c5 2.♘f3 ♘c6 3.d4 cxd4 4.♘xd4 g6 5.♘c3 ♗g7 6.♗e3 d6 7.♕d2 ♘f6 8.f3 0-0 9.♗c4 a5 10.h4 ♘e5 11.♗e2

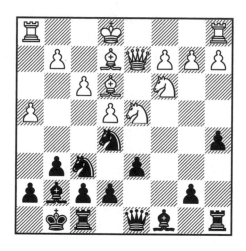

White abandons control of the a2-g8 diagonal in favor of fortifying his center. This is a logical line for White against an early ...a7-a5. Stubbornly holding onto the diagonal often allows Black to kick the bishop around with tempo during the attack. Having examined that theme in some of our earlier games, let's see how easy the safer plan is for White.

11...a4 12.a3

Let's take a moment to examine the pawn structure prior to this move. White's pawns at c2, b2, and a2 are strongest when standing on their original squares. That is not specific to this game – it is general chess theory that pawns are strongest on their original squares. White's decision to play a2-a3 weakens the pawn structure, yet failure to make this move allows Black to get his own pawn to a3 first, which is a less attractive option for White. An examination of the structure c2/b2/a3 shows that it is stronger than the structure c2/b3/a2. So White decides on a2-a3 because, in addition to the issue of the weakened pawns, the black bishop's potential power over the long a1-h8 diagonal is increased if the b-pawn moves.

12...♕a5 13.0-0-0 ♗d7

White connects the rooks before launching his kingside attack, and Black places the bishop on d7 to prepare the ...b7-b5 pawn push.

14.♗h6 b5 15.♗xg7 ♔xg7 16.h5 b4

The Dragon player does best not to overreact to the threat of ♗h6 followed by the white pawns' advance. Often, an active defense leads to Black's downfall, as in 16...♘xh5 17.g4 ♘f6 18.♕h6+ ♔g8 19.♘d5, when Black is completely lost: his f6-knight can no longer both safeguard h7 and deal with the d5-knight.

17.axb4 ♕xb4 18.hxg6 fxg6 19.♕h6+ ♔f7

Take note of how passive defense created a natural escape path via f7 to e8.

20.♘a2 ♕b6 21.f4 ♖fb8

The choice of the king's rook to b8 is significant. It indicates that Black is not afraid of White's kingside attack and that Black is moving in for the kill himself. Moving the queen's rook to b8 would also threaten b2 and leaving the rook at f8 provides a little more safety for the king as it is shielded from back-rank checks.

22.♗b5

This is not so much a blunder as it is frustration with the fact that all options are bad, for example 22.fxe5 ♕xb2+ 23.♔d2 ♕xd4+ 24.♔e1 ♕xe5 25.♗c4+ ♗e6 26.♗xe6+ ♕xe6 27.♘c3 a3 and Black is completely winning.

22...♘eg4 23.♕g5 ♗xb5 24.e5 ♗d7 25.e6+ ♗xe6 26.♘c3 ♕xb2+ 27.♔d2 ♕xc3+ 0-1

After 28.♔xc3 ♘e4+ Black regains the queen, coming out with an extra piece and a very strong passed pawn.

Game 37

Smetana, Jaroslav – Jirovský, Petr [B77]
Czechoslovakia Team Chp 1991

In the previous game, GM Miloš Jirovský played the black pieces. In this game, his brother, IM Petr Jirovský, has Black – and there is another brother, IM Pavel Jirovský, who is also known to play 9...a5 in the Dragon!

1.e4 c5 2.♘f3 d6 3.d4 cxd4 4.♘xd4 ♘f6 5.♘c3 g6 6.♗e3 ♗g7 7.f3 0-0 8.♕d2 ♘c6 9.♗c4 a5 10.♘db5

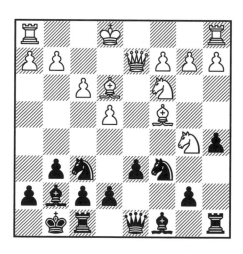

White drops his knight on b5 to slow down Black's progress on the queenside. This is very much a passive approach to dealing with ...a7-a5.

10...a4 11.a3 ♘e5 12.♗e2 ♗d7 13.0-0 ♕a5

The Yugoslav Attack is defined by pawns on f3 and e4, queen at d2, and bishop at e3, along with queenside castling. If White is afraid to castle long, he needs to question his choice of lines against the Dragon.

14.♕e1 ♖fc8 15.♕f2

Two queen moves in a row telegraph the threat of ♗e3-b6 forcing the queen to a6 and unleashing ♘b5-c7! trapping the queen. Black will have none of this silliness and sees beyond the short-term threat.

15...♗xb5!

Now on 16.♘xb5 ♖xc2 17.♘d4 ♖xb2, Black enjoys a pawn buffet and a winning position. Or if 16.♗xb5 ♖xc3 17.bxc3 ♕xb5 18.♖ab1 ♕d7, Black is again winning. All that remains is the original plan of trapping the queen.

16.♗b6 ♗xe2!

Black refutes the trapping idea by correctly evaluating the power of the minor pieces and rook versus a queen.

17.♗xa5 ♗xf1 18.♖xf1 ♖xa5

Black has a bishop, knight, and rook for the queen. As a general rule, the answer to who is stronger, a rook and two minor pieces or a queen, is "it depends on the position." In a pawnless ending, I've read that rook and two minor pieces versus a queen is a draw. There are many positions where rook, one minor piece and a pawn are enough compensation. Sadly, I once had the queen in a simultaneous game against Anatoly Karpov and lost. In the current position, Black has a clear advantage.

19.♕b6 ♖aa8

Black understands that the temporary loss of the b-pawn is not an issue. His pieces are placed well and the semi-open files will work to his advantage very quickly.

20.♕xb7 ♔f8 21.♘d5 ♘xd5 22.♕xd5 ♘c4

Black simultaneously threatens forking rook and queen at e3 and taking the pawn at b2. White could play 23.♕b5, but then Black would simply play 23...♗xb2 instead of ...♘xb2 and White's position is still crumbling.

23.♖e1 ♘xb2 24.f4

White hopes to advance the pawn and decrease the scope of Black's minor pieces. In truth, he is just going through the motions before resigning. He is thinking, "I play these moves and if you respond correctly I resign. If not, I might slip back into the game again..."

24...♘c4

Black will brook no nonsense and shuts White down with excellent technique.

25.e5 e6 26.♕b5 dxe5 27.fxe5 ♔g8 28.♖e4 ♘xa3

This would be a fine place to resign, as the passed pawn is very powerful.

29.♕d7 ♘c4 30.♕b7 ♖cb8 0-1

White cannot stop the advancing pawn from queening.

9...♛a5

Game 38

Äijälä, Jouko – Ljubojević, Ljubomir [B79]
World U26 Team Chp, Dresden 1969

**1.e4 c5 2.♞f3 d6 3.d4 cxd4 4.♞xd4 ♞f6 5.♞c3 ♞c6 6.♗c4
♗d7 7.♗b3 g6 8.f3 ♗g7**

Modern Dragon players normally go about the business of fianchettoing the bishop with ...g7-g6 and ...♗f8-g7 before playing ...♗c8-d7.

9.♗e3 ♛a5

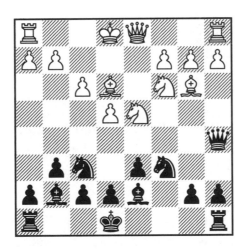

Worthy of our consideration and study is ...♗c8-d7 before castling, in conjunction with 9...♛a5. This way, Black creates a tremendous amount of flexibility in his position; he may even consider leaving his king in the center if the right conditions arise.

10.♛d2 0-0 11.0-0-0 ♜fc8

White has created a standard Yugoslav position, but that does not mean 0-0-0 should be played out of obligation. No, White should objectively look at the position and decide if it is wise to forgo castling into the fire. A strategic attribute of ...♕d8-a5 is the ability to place the king's rook on c8. This allows both rooks to participate in the game much earlier than in many other Dragon variations.

12.h4 ♘e5 13.g4 b5

A good general rule is to remember that castling on opposite wings creates an all-out war, while castling short creates a bore. Do you want to be bored, or to go to war?

14.h5 ♘c4

Black could have easily justified kicking the opposing knight with 14...b4 instead of dropping his own knight into c4. However, he has a different idea for the attack.

15.♗xc4 bxc4!

Black creates a powerful semi-open file, while the c4-pawn restricts White from advancing his b-pawn.

16.hxg6 fxg6

After 16...hxg6, Black is in immediate trouble after 17.♗h6.

17.♕h2 ♖ab8 18.♘d5 c3!

Black is not impressed by the threat of ♘xf6+ and the potential of ♕xh7 with check. Playing ...c4-c3 here demonstrates that he is confident his attack will pay off first. Is he correct? Looks pretty dangerous for both sides.

19.♘xf6+ exf6 20.♕xh7+ ♔f7 21.♘f5?? gxf5

White tossed the game away when he failed to find the devilish move 21.♖h6! which should turn the tables and give White the upper hand after 21.♖h6 ♕xa2 22.♕xg6+ ♔f8 23.bxc3 ♕a1+ 24.♔d2 ♕xc3+ 25.♔e2 ♕c4+ 26.♔f2 ♕f7 27.♕xf7+ ♔xf7 28.♖h5.

22.♖xd6 cxb2+ 23.♔b1 ♕a4 24.♖d2 ♖h8 0-1

Game 39

Seck, A. – Velásquez, Manuel [B79]
Dubai Olympiad 1986

1.e4 c5 2.♘f3 d6 3.d4 cxd4 4.♘xd4 ♘f6 5.♘c3 g6 6.♗e3 ♗g7 7.f3 ♗d7 8.♕d2 ♘c6 9.♗c4 ♕a5 10.♘de2 0-0 11.0-0-0

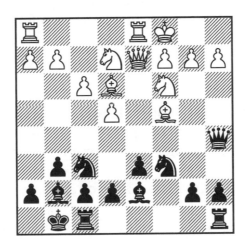

11...♖fc8

As mentioned in the previous game, one of the benefits of an early ...♕d8-a5 is that the rooks become connected very quickly.

12.♗b3 ♘e5 13.♗h6

Preferable is 13.♔b1, improving the security of the king before White travels abroad. A common device for Black is to retreat the bishop to h8 so as not to allow the exchange. As Black, every time I am faced with the prospect of ♗h6, I ask myself, *"can and should I play ...♗h8?"* I take this rule to such an extreme that I even ask the question if my rook is still on f8 and doing so would drop an exchange. Here, Black has another idea.

13...♞c4

It is tempting for Black to draw the queen away from the defense of the king with 13...♝xh6, yet it is also hard to find an advantage in doing so. 13...♝xh6 14.♕xh6 b5 15.♚b1 b4 16.♞d5 ♞xd5 17.♝xd5 ♕c7 18.♞d4 is equal.

14.♝xc4 ♖xc4 15.h4 ♖ac8

Doubling the rooks on the c-file is an optimal Dragon pattern, yet White's connected knights at e2 and c3 offer solid resistance.

16.h5 ♞xe4

As we have seen in many games, the pattern of sacrificing a knight at g4 or e4 is a common theme for launching an attack. If you embed the search for these kinds of opportunities into your DNA, you'll win some spectacular games over your chess career.

17.fxe4 ♝xc3 18.♞xc3 ♖xc3 19.bxc3

As promising as this looks, White should be able to hold Black off.

19...♕a3+ 20.♚b1 ♝e6?

Black needs to draw the white bishop back with 20...♖c6!, forcing 21.♝e3 to deny the rook the b6 square. What might appear to be a minor nuance in the move order is enough for Black to lose now. Proper play would continue along the lines of 20...♖c6 21.♝e3 ♝e6 22.c4 ♖xc4 23.c3 ♖xc3 24.hxg6 ♖xe3 25.gxh7+ ♚h8 26.♕d4+ f6 27.♖d2 b6 28.♖c2 ♖d3 29.♕b2 ♕a5, with equal chances.

21.c4 ♖xc4 22.♖h3??

Here, 22.c3 is the only way to play for the win, but the position is complex with many twists and turns: 22.c3 ♖c5 23.♖c1 ♖b5+ 24.♚a1

♗xa2 25.♕xa2 ♕c5 26.hxg6 hxg6 27.♗e3 ♕c7 28.♖h8+ ♔xh8 29.♕xf7 ♕a5+ 30.♕a2 ♕xa2+ 31.♔xa2 ♔g8. White is clearly better, but who knows how much witchcraft is left in these lines?

22...♗xh3 23.gxh3 ♖b4+ 0-1

Game 40

Ermakov, Alexander – Hamburg [B75]
Soviet Army Chp 1972

1.e4 c5 2.♘f3 d6 3.d4 cxd4 4.♘xd4 ♘f6 5.♘c3 g6 6.♗e3 ♗g7 7.f3 ♘c6 8.♗c4 ♗d7 9.♗b3 ♕a5 10.♕d2 ♘e5 11.♗h6

Normally, when Black is faced with this pattern, he castles king-side in order to recapture with his king on g7. Black decides to throw caution to the wind.

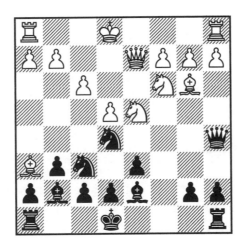

11...♗xh6

I often wonder in these situations if White regrets forcing the line. Now Black has stated he has no fear of keeping his king in the center and the only justification can be that Black plans to deliver checkmate before getting mated himself.

12.♕xh6 ♖c8

Black correctly develops his rook, as he has nothing to fear on the kingside. If White tries to rush in and deprive Black of the right to castle, he will pay a high price for it. After 13.♕g7 ♖g8 14.♕h6 g5, White's best play is to give up his queen for the rook after ...♖g6. Attempts at extracting the queen with f3-f4 end up far worse.

13.0-0-0 ♖xc3 14.bxc3 ♕xc3

Probably the most common theme Dragon players have in their toolbox is the exchange sacrifice at c3. It can become such an addiction for the Dragon player that if material is even, he feels he is losing!

15.♘e2 ♘d3+

White has learned why ♔b1 is often played before rushing off to attack Black. The disruptive ...♘d3+ is a good theme for the novice player to learn, as it is easy to overlook this during a game.

16.♖xd3 ♕a1+ 17.♔d2 ♕xh1

Let's take inventory and recall that Black sacrificed an exchange to win an exchange. His position is good, but it is far from an overwhelming victory.

18.g4 ♕g2 19.h4 ♗xg4

Black can make progress without resorting to complications. There is nothing wrong with normal ideas like 19...♗c6 20.♕e3 0-0 21.♕xa7 ♕h2, when Black is OK.

20.fxg4?

White fails to find the saving resource 20.♕g7, the point being that the rook must move to f8 to protect the f-pawn, creating the tactical possibility of ♗b3-a4+ driving the king away from protecting the rook: 20.♕g7 ♖f8 21.fxg4 ♘xe4+ 22.♔c1 ♘c5 (22...♕xe2? 23.♗a4+) 23.♖e3 ♕xg4 24.♔b2 ♕xh4 25.♘c3, and the position is roughly equal.

20...♞xe4+ 21.♚e3? ♛f2+ 22.♚xe4 f5+ 23.gxf5 gxf5+ 24.♚d5 ♛c5+ 0-1

White's least bad option was to play 21.♚c1, dropping the e2-knight, which of course is also losing but not as quickly as mate! After 24...♛c5+, the game ends with 25.♚e6 ♛e5#.

Game 41

Mnatsakanian, Eduard – Veresov, Gavriil [B79]
USSR 1968

1.e4 c5 2.♞f3 ♞c6 3.d4 cxd4 4.♞xd4 g6

The Accelerated Dragon move order, with an early ...g7-g6 prior to ...d7-d6, often allows for ...d7-d5 in one move, with an advantage for Black.

5.♞c3 ♝g7 6.♝e3 ♞f6 7.♝c4 d6 8.f3 0-0 9.♛d2 ♝d7 10.♝b3 ♛a5

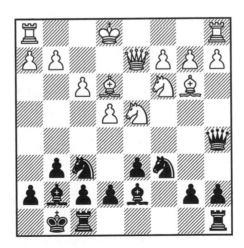

This game is a good example of how ...♛d8-a5 plays out in normalized main-line-type formations. By delaying the queen sortie to move 10, we review a different slice of the ideas a tad closer to a main-line Dragon.

11.0-0-0 ♕fc8

Black's army aims at the queenside, waiting for the order to fire.

12.g4 ♘e5 13.h4 ♖c4

Black offers the exchange, not to eliminate the dark-squared bishop but to anchor the knight on the powerful c4 square. I'm going to share a speed-chess trick that I've used and one that I suspect many GMs and strong players have also used. When I'm facing a very strong player, he might take 15 to 20 seconds and play ...♖c4 here, upon which I would instantly play 14.g5. The crazy speed-chess logic is that if he's offered up the exchange, it must be good for him if I take it, whereas if I play a direct attacking move, almost instantly he'll think that I saw all of his plans and crush his spirit. If you think this is foolish, I have heard top-ranked players admit they've done the same thing. I do not recommend this in tournament play, but in speed chess it's a nice tool to have at your disposal.

14.♗xc4

As they say in the movies, sometimes speed chess imitates life. (Well, they don't really say that, but you know what I mean...) White's best plan is to ignore the offer of the exchange and play aggressively. After 14.g5 ♘h5 15.f4 ♖xd4 16.♕xd4 ♘g4 17.e5 ♘g3 18.♖he1 ♘f5 19.♕d5 ♕xd5 20.♘xd5 e6 21.♗g1 exd5 22.♗xd5 ♖b8 23.♗xa7 ♖a8 24.♗g1, White has the advantage.

After the text move, Black is the exchange down but close to equal positionally and with potential tricks.

14...♘xc4 15.♕d3 b5 16.♘b3 ♕a6 17.♗d4 e5!

I give 17...e5 an exclamation mark because it is psychologically very difficult for a Dragon player to block in his dark-squared bishop.

18.♗f2

Instead of retreating the bishop, White could create complications with 18.♗c5!?. If White does choose this path, he must be careful not to take a materialistic approach to the position, as 18.♝c5 dxc5 19.♞xc5 ♛a5 20.♞xd7 ♛b4 21.♞xf6+ ♝xf6 22.♖df1 ♛xb2+ 23.♚d1 favors Black slightly.

18...b4 19.♞d5 ♞xd5 20.♛xd5 ♝c6 21.♛d3 ♝b5

White should seek a draw with 22.♛d5 ♝c6 23.♛d3 ♝b5 and force Black to find a different plan. One possibility is 22.♛d5 ♛xa2 23.♛xa8+ ♝f8 24.♖d5 ♛xb2+ 25.♚d1 ♛b1+ 26.♞c1 ♝a4 27.♚e2 ♛xc2+ 28.♚f1 ♝c6, and now White's best move may very well be 29.♛xc6 allowing the discovered attack 29...♞d2+, as moving the queen to safety permits Black to remove the rook and pry White's position open for the attack.

22.♞d2??

White's horrible move is quickly punished. Two general patterns to keep in mind here are not to build a box of pieces around your king and not to allow discovered attacks. Now, after the discovered attack, White no longer has d2 available as a retreat square.

22...♞xb2 23.♛d5

The discovery pushes the queen further away from the king's defense. Of course, he can't take the knight, as the bishop is attacking the queen on d3.

23...♞d3+ 24.♚b1

The knight fails to offer any real resistance: 24.cxd3 ♛a3+ 25.♚b1 ♝xd3+ 26.♛xd3 ♛xd3+ 27.♚a1 ♖c8 28.♞b3 ♛xf3, and Black's position is crushing.

24...♛a3 0-1

White's only defense drops material: 25.♛b3 ♛xb3+ 26.axb3 ♞xf2 27.♖hg1 ♞xd1 28.♖xd1−+.

9.♗c4 ♗d7 10.0-0-0 ♖b8

Game 42

Bitoon, Richard (2476) – So, Wesley (2665) [B77]
Philippines Chp 2010

1.e4 c5 2.♘f3 d6 3.d4 cxd4 4.♘xd4 ♘f6 5.♘c3 g6 6.♗e3 ♗g7 7.f3 0-0 8.♕d2 ♘c6 9.♗c4 ♗d7 10.0-0-0 ♖b8

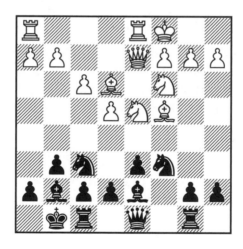

The historical main-line Dragon finds the rook on c8 with pressure on the semi-open file. With ...♖a8-b8 instead, Black intends to use his b-pawn as a battering ram to open up White's castle.

11.♗b3

I would strongly advise White not to go pawn-grabbing with 11.♘xc6 bxc6 12.♗xa7 ♖b7 13.♗e3 ♕a5. While it is true that there is no immediate threat, the margin of error is very small for White, and a small mistake could bring disaster.

11...♘a5 12.h4 b5

In the main-line Dragon, Black can often get this push in via a sacrifice, but with the early ...♖a8-b8, he can play ...b7-b5 as often as a rerun movie on HBO.

13.♔b1 ♘c4

Yes, ...b5-b4 is also a theme seen in the Dragon. However, as a general observation, it has more power when a set of knights has been traded off or when the move forces a trade. Black's plan here is to gain a semi-open file against b2, which is a difficult square to defend.

14.♗xc4 bxc4 15.g4 ♕b6

Black threatens mate on b2, so White must choose between 16.♕c1 and 16.b3. The passive queen move blocks the king into a small box, so 16.b3 is objectively better. It is a natural reaction for White to reject this idea due to the fear of the long a1-h8 diagonal.

16.♕c1 ♕a5

White having played the weaker 16.♕c1, Black jumps on the position with the threat of ...♕xc3.

17.♔a1

The defensive idea 17.♘de2 runs into trouble after 17...♗xg4 18.fxg4 ♘xe4 19.♗d4 ♗xd4 20.♖xd4 ♘xc3+ 21.♘xc3 ♕xc3 22.♖dd1 f5 23.gxf5 ♖xf5, and Black's superior pawns are enough to bring home the full point even if his queenside attack evaporates.

17...♖b6

If Black sneaks the rook over to a6, he may eventually have a mate threat at a2.

18.♘de2 ♖b7

After the d4-knight's retreat, Black decides that the target on a2 is less attractive, as the knights have "doubled' on the c3 square.

Therefore, he moves the rook in order to avoid getting with a sudden ♘c3-d5. However, it's hard to imagine that White would move the knight and free up the approaches to b2.

19.g5

White's choice is too slow to generate counterplay. Better is 19.♗h6 ♖fb8 20.♗xg7 ♔xg7, when White is equal after the dynamic 21.♕g5!.

19...♘h5 20.♕d2?

What madness is this? For better or worse, the white queen must remain on c1 and wait for the change of seasons. Harassing the opposing queen with 20.♖d5 or challenging the bishop with 20.♗d4 are better options.

20...♖fb8 21.♖b1

White has now earned a Ph.D. in violating our rule of not boxing yourself in. Black's primary target is b2, but a2 is weak so Black should search for hidden ways to exploit it.

21...♘g3

Once again, from the other side of the board the knight diverts pieces away from the center in order to pry the game open. The novice player will have a difficult time defending against moves like this, as they seem to appear out of nowhere. However, by now you should have a feel for the flying black knight.

22.♘xg3

White could try 22.♗d4 ♘xh1 23.♗xg7 ♔xg7 24.♕d1 ♗a4 (not 24...♘xf2 25.♕d4+) 25.♘xa4 ♕xa4 26.♘c3 ♕a5 27.♕xh1 ♖xb2 28.♖xb2 ♕xc3 29.♕c1 e5 30.♔b1 ♖xb2+ 31.♕xb2 ♕xf3. However, Black is still winning.

22...♖xb2 23.♗d4 ♖xa2+

Black has finished off White thanks to the weak a2 square. It's like Indiana Jones and the Temple of Doom, and we have found the Holy Grail. The queen must fall. White most likely played 23.♗d4 without thinking, once he realized that 23.♖xb2 is crushed by 23...♗xc3. However, it all ends the same way.

24.♘xa2 ♖xb1+ 0-1

Game 43

Könnyű, János (2382) – Sedlak, Nikola (2550) [B78]
Hungarian Chp 2011

1.e4 c5 2.♘f3 d6 3.d4 cxd4 4.♘xd4 ♘f6 5.♘c3 g6 6.♗e3 ♗g7 7.f3 0-0 8.♕d2 ♘c6 9.♗c4 ♗d7 10.0-0-0 ♖b8 11.♖he1

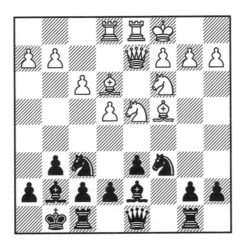

The moment I saw this move, I cringed. Why not 11.♔b1 or 11.♗b3 ? What positive attribute does this move contain? Is White trying to anchor down on e4 to stop the flying knights on move 25? If so, he is seeing ghosts and needs to deal with the present.

11...b5 12.♗b3 ♘e5

Because of White's foolish move, it's as if Black has gained a tempo for the attack.

13.♗h6 ♗xh6

White has gotten rid of the dangerous Dragon bishop, but can he make it back in time to defend the queenside?

14.♕xh6 a5

A common pattern is the pawn swarm that traps the light-squared bishop. Sometimes they look trapped up to the very last second and then wriggle free; sometimes all you can get for your piece is a pawn and a check. Regardless, it's time for White to go into a deep think and make the right choice.

15.a4?

This is not the right choice to open lines up against the king.

White could try to fight his way out of this mess like a boxer, using 15.f4 ♘eg4 16.♕h4 a4 17.e5 axb3 18.♘xb3 ♘h5 19.h3 ♘xf4 20.exd6 exd6 21.♕xd8 ♖fxd8 22.hxg4. However, Black is still better and boxers sometimes get knocked out.

Alternatively, White could try the wriggling idea with 15.h3 a4 16.f4 axb3 17.fxe5 bxa2 18.♘xa2 dxe5 19.♘c6 ♗xc6 20.♖xd8 ♖fxd8 21.b3. Before we get too excited for White here, let me add that I'm sure Black could improve in this line, and ironically, he hardly needs to worry as Black probably has solid compensation in this position and is at least equal if not better.

15...bxa4 16.♗xa4 ♕b6

White has an abundance of weak squares and Black has the direct threat of mate on b2.

17.b3 ♕b4 18.♘de2

Better is 18.♖e3 to defend the knight, when by doing so we can try to justify the horrible move 11.♖he1.

18...♗xa4 0-1

124

9.♗c4 ♗d7 10.0-0-0 ♖b8

It is disappointing to see someone resign before "the move" is played. No worries, though, as White is completely lost here. Had White played 19.♘xa4, we would have our magical ...♘d3+ again, similar to Game 40, while 19.♖d4 ♕a3+ 20.♔b1 ♗xb3 is crushing and quickly ends in mate.

Game 44

Chen Fan (2354) – Bu Xiangzhi (2630) [B78]
Torch Cup, Xiapu (China) 2005

1.e4 c5 2.♘f3 d6 3.d4 cxd4 4.♘xd4 ♘f6 5.♘c3 g6 6.♗e3 ♗g7 7.f3 ♘c6 8.♕d2 0-0 9.0-0-0 ♗d7 10.♗c4 ♖b8 11.♘b3

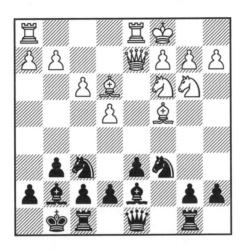

White decides early on that he won't fall for any tricks on b2, so he plants the knight on b3. A noble idea, but what does one do with the c4-bishop then? The astute student will observe that ♗f1-c4 was played prior to ...♖a8-b8, but yet by the very act of not having a square for the bishop, it's as if ...♖a8-b8 came for free. If theory said 10.♘b3 is a good move here, I would still have a hard time playing these ideas for White. You need to understand the moves you play and why you are playing them. It's not all about reading an opening manual that says if "x" goes here, I must do "y" because that's the next move in the book. Sometimes it's the simple, "Today I shall plant an apple tree, and I'll put it here because it will receive plenty of sun and have easy access to water."

11...♘a5 12.♗e2

Black immediately puts the question to the bishop, and White plays along by dropping the bishop back. The question is, Why? If he took time to reflect upon our observations on the previous move, he should consider 12.♘xa5 ♕xa5 13.♘d5 ♕xd2+ 14.♖xd2 ♘xd5 15.exd5 when White is at least equal. Often, the challenge in chess is that our pride won't allow us to change direction, even if we know that doing so will improve our journey.

12...b5 13.♗xa7 ♖a8

White's pawn-grabbing is a classic case of delusions of grandeur. I can't imagine by what measure clearing a file against his king could be considered a good idea.

14.♗d4 ♘c4 15.♕e1

Capturing the black knight on c4 kicks the white b3-knight to an awkward square: 15.♗xc4 bxc4 16.♘a1. Therefore, White opts for retreat.

15...♕c7 16.♔b1

The king can now do his fair share to help support the a2 square, but this hardly ends his problems.

16...e5

I have great respect for players who can overcome the mental block to close in their Dragon bishop in the heat of battle. Here Black does so in preparation for attacking the queenside.

17.♗f2 ♘xb2

The tactical point behind Black's blocking in his bishop is to prevent White's ♗d4 and therefore to further weaken the opposing king.

18.♔xb2 b4

The last two moves are the only logical ones in the position.

19.♖d3

The knight cannot move from the c3 square: 19.♘d5 ♖xa2+ 20.♔xa2 ♕xc2+ 21.♔a1 ♖a8+ and, after giving away his pieces on the a-file, White gets mated.

19...d5 20.exd5 e4

Black quickly clears a path for the bishop to come back to life. The opening of this line is devastating. White must search hard for a reason not to resign right here.

21.d6

If I intended to play on, I would challenge the bishop with 21.♗d4. However, 21.d6 is only slightly worse, while capturing the pawn 21.fxe4 ♘xe4 22.♔b1 ♘xc3+ 23.♖xc3 bxc3 offers White nothing.

21...♕c6 22.♘d4 ♕c4

Nonchalantly putting your queen on a square where White can execute a discovered attack is just a subtle way of saying, "Resign now, please!"

23.♘a4 exd3 24.♗xd3 ♕d5 0-1

Game 45

Hakki, Imad (2433) – Kojima, Shinya (2187) [B77]
Doha (rapid) 2006

1.e4 c5 2.♘c3 ♘c6 3.♘f3 g6 4.d4 cxd4 5.♘xd4 ♗g7 6.♗e3 ♘f6 7.♗c4 d6 8.f3 0-0 9.♕d2 ♗d7 10.0-0-0 ♖b8 11.♗b3 ♘a5 12.♗h6

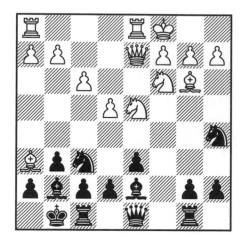

This is a popular line in response to ...♖a8-b8; in fact an early ♗e3-h6 against the Dragon is a theme for White in many lines. It provides White the advantage of taking the Dragon bishop off the board before Black moves his king's rook, after which ♗e3-h6 can be answered by ...♗g7-h8. The downside is that the traveling queen is often called back to defend her king.

12...♗xh6 13.♕xh6 b5

As the thematic idea of ...♖a8-b8 is to play an early ...b7-b5, it is often played at the first opportunity.

14.♔b1 e5

White must play fast on the kingside in order to justify his queen's placement at h6. The idea of g2-g4 here and trying to bust Black open is more in harmony with the early queen move. Black takes advantage of White's passive move 14 to push the enemy knight off d4 and relegate it to a less active post.

15.♘de2 ♘xb3 16.axb3 b4 17.♘a4

I prefer 17.♘d5, holding the d5 square. With 17.♘a4, White is playing into Black's attack.

17...♗xa4 18.bxa4 b3 19.♕d2 bxc2+

The queen had no choice: she had to come back and seal the gap created by 17.♘a4. Black has a good position and should pile on the pressure with his major pieces.

20.♕xc2 ♕b6

The question I ask myself when considering whether to double my major pieces is, *Do I want to lead with my queen or with my rooks?* Leading with the rooks could be accomplished thus: 20...♕d7 21.♘c3 ♖fc8 22.♖d3 ♖c6 23.♖hd1 ♖cb6 24.♖3d2 a6 25.♕d3 ♕b7 26.♕e2. However, there is nothing wrong with 20...♕b6 – it's a fine move.

21.♘c3 ♖fc8 22.g4?

One of the worst crimes you can commit in chess is forcing your opponent to find a good idea. White must be thinking g4-g5 and forcing the knight off f6, but why? Yes, it's guarding d5 but it can do more important things and, with this encouragement, Black will find them!

22...♖c4 23.g5 ♘d7 24.♖d2 ♘c5

White needs two rooks to defend and he needs them quickly. 24.♖he1 or the more aggressive 24.♖d5 would provide more resistance in a very tough position. Without a doubt, 22.g4 and 23.g5 are the losing moves, as they contribute nothing to White's game.

25.♖hd1 ♕a5 26.♖xd6

The game is over, but White has yet to figure this out. We should not view White's pawn grab as reckless; the idea here is if we can get a check on the back rank to create a trick, it's about all we have so let's play it before we resign.

26...♖xc3! 27.♕d2

I don't think White saw the next move, else he may have tried 27.♖d8+ to mix things up.

27...♖xb2+! 28.♔xb2 ♕b4+ 0-1

Here 28.♕xb2 prolongs the game, but after 28...♖b3 it's still an easy win. White resigned in the final position because mate is unstoppable, for example 29.♔a1 ♕a3+ 30.♕a2 ♖c1+ 31.♖xc1 ♘b3+ 32.♔b1 ♕xc1#.

Game 46

Domínguez Pérez, Leinier (2717) – Carlsen, Magnus (2776) [B77]
Linares 2009

1.e4 c5 2.♘f3 d6 3.d4 cxd4 4.♘xd4 ♘f6 5.♘c3 g6 6.♗e3 ♗g7 7.f3 ♘c6 8.♕d2 0-0 9.♗c4 ♗d7 10.0-0-0 ♖b8

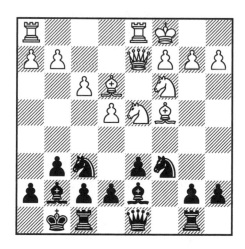

If 10...♖b8 is worthy of being part of a world champion's repertoire, it should be one of the tools at your disposal too.

11.♗b3 ♘a5 12.♗h6 ♗xh6 13.♕xh6 b5 14.g4

In Game 45, White played 14.♔b1 and Black quickly gained an advantage after 14...e5. The very purpose of 14.g4 is to prevent Black from playing ...e7-e5.

14...♘xb3+

Here 14...e5? fails, as 15.♘f5! ♗xf5 16.exf5 ♔h8 17.♘e4 ♘xb3+ 18.axb3 ♘xe4 19.fxe4 ♖g8 yields White a strong edge.

15.♘xb3 b4 16.♘d5 ♘xd5 17.exd5 ♖b6!

Until this game, the most popular move here was 17...♕c7, with mixed results. World Champion Carlsen is credited with discovering this move and with creating the realization that the line is good for Black. However, a year prior to this game, a relatively unknown Israeli WIM named Maya Porat played 17...♖b6 against GM Konstantin Maslak at the Pardubice Open in 2008 and ended up with a very solid position. In fact, Porat was ahead for most of the game and was only outplayed in a tricky ending. The idea of 17...♖b6 is to protect the d-pawn so that Black can play ...e7-e5 and recapture with the f-pawn on e6. This is exactly how Porat played the game. Did he influence Carlsen? We will never know for sure, but I suspect a world champion takes note of such developments.

18.♖he1

White pulls his rook to the center to apply pressure against the pawn advance that he knows is coming. In Maslak–Porat, White tried 18.h4 e5 19.dxe6 fxe6 20.♖d3 ♗b5 21.♖e3 e5 22.h5 g5 23.♕e6+ ♔h8 24.♘d2 ♗d7 25.♕d5 and Black played for the win with 25...♕e7. However, as a 400-point underdog she might have tried to repeat the position and draw with 25...♗c6 26.♕d3 ♕f6 27.♔b1 ♗b5 28.♕d5 ♗c6 29.♕d3 ♗b5, etc.

18...e5 19.dxe6 fxe6 20.♖e3

I do not like 20.♖e3 as it blocks the queen's path. If White wants to play in the center, he should consider pulling his queen back to participate in the game. This seems to be White's best idea here, as trying to leave the queen on h6 to attack on the wing doesn't work: 20.f4 ♕f6 21.♖d4 ♖c8 22.♖ed1 ♖bc6 23.♖1d2 e5 24.♖xb4 ♗xg4 25.♕g5 ♕xg5 26.fxg5, and White is on the fast lane to a losing ending.

20...♖f7

I prefer the straightforward 20...e5, whereas the World Champion decides to take a moment and protect the seventh rank. It's hard to see into the mind of a world-class player but my guess is that he's waiting for White to commit to a plan with his knight before deciding how to arrange his pawns.

21.♘d2 d5

Black cuts down on the white knight's scope, controlling the e3 and c4 squares.

22.♘b3

On the face of it, it might appear the knight return to b3 means that White lacks a plan. That's not the case at all, however – Black held back his pawns until White forced him to commit by playing ♘d2 and now with the knight returning the first player wants to capitalize on the dark-square weakness created by the d-pawn's advance. If you imagine a tennis match with two strong players volleying back and forth, that's sort of what just happened here. The challenge for White is how to protect the king while exploiting the dark squares. It's becoming clear that 20.♖e3, blocking the queen's retreat, is going to cost White.

22...♕c7 23.♔b1

If White tries a pawn storm, Black has a nice resource: 23.h4 ♗a4 24.h5 ♗xb3 25.♖xb3 ♕f4+, trading queens and still keeping an edge in the ending.

23...♖b8 24.♖de1

I don't like White's move at all – this may have been his last chance to activate the queen with 24.♕h4 ♖bf8 25.♕f2 ♖f4 26.♕e2 ♕b6 27.♘d2 when, while Black is better, White is at least in the game.

24...♖c8 25.♖1e2 ♕b6 26.h4

9.♗c4 ♗d7 10.0-0-0 ♖b8

This is almost a desperation attack as Black has complete control of the center.

26...d4! 27.♖e5

Of course, 27.♖d3 is impossible because of 27...♗b5!.

27...d3!!

Psychologically speaking, this is a crushing move, the moment where you realize your opponent is opening you up like a tin can.

28.cxd3 ♖xf3 29.d4?

This move is bewildering: how long will White play on a queen down? Correct is 29.♕d2 and now all his pieces can play chess together. It's very hard to understand how a 2700+ player could miss this, but it goes back to what I mentioned previously about assessing the position. Many times a game is lost, not because a player failed to see far enough ahead or because he missed something along the way, but because he incorrectly evaluated the final position that both players visualized at the end of a variation. If both players believe that they are winning nine moves ahead and they reach the expected position, it is impossible for both players to be correct and winning. Oddly enough, both players can believe they are winning and be wrong as it's an even or drawn position; however, both can never be correct in believing that they are winning.

29...♗b5

Crushing; if 30.♖xe6 ♕xe6 31.♖xe6 ♗d3+ 32.♔a1 ♖f1+; or 30.♖e1 ♖xb3! 31.axb3 ♗d3+ 32.♔a2 ♕a6+.

30.♖2e3 ♗d3+ 31.♔a1 ♕xd4

A very good move, but later a computer found that Carlsen missed a faster win with 31...♖f2 32.♖e1 ♖xb2 33.♔xb2 ♖c2+ 34.♔a1 ♕c6 35.♖c5 ♖xa2+ 36.♔xa2 ♕a4+ 37.♔b2 ♕a3#. To be fair to the World

Champion, 31...♖f2 is not a natural-looking move, it's easy to see how it was missed with nine moves to reach the time control.

32.♖xe6

If 32.♘xd4? ♖c1 is checkmate.

The rest of the game is a clinic in high-level technique.

32...♖f1+ 33.♖e1 ♕xg4 34.♖xf1 ♕xe6 35.♘c5 ♕e2 36.♖c1 ♗f5 37.♕f4 a5 38.h5 ♕e7 39.♕c4+ ♗e6

White missed an opportunity to mix things up with 39.hxg6 ♖xc5 40.gxh7+ ♔xh7 41.♕h2+; this idea is so risky for Black that he should just recapture 39.hxg6 hxg6.

40.♕c2 ♕g5 41.hxg6 hxg6

The pinned knight is an overwhelming weakness: White is lost.

42.a3

White's position is so bad that resignation comes strongly into consideration. He boldly tries to carry on with 42.a3, but there is a time in chess when your position is such that you might as well swing for the fences. My swing here would be 42.♕b1 ♖xc5 43.♖xc5 ♕xc5 44.♕xg6+ ♔f8 45.♕h7 ♔e8 46.♕h8+ ♔e7 47.♕h4+ ♔d7 48.♕h7+ ♔c6 49.♕e4+ ♔c7 50.♕f4+ ♔b6 51.♕b8+ ♔c6 52.♕a8+ ♔c7 53.♕h1. Yes, White is lost, but Black cannot win with a rook pawn as the queening square is not the same color as his bishop's. It's about all White has, and with many checks and queen moves there are many lines and ideas and therefore chances for Black to slip up.

42...bxa3 43.♕c3

Sadly, White cannot recapture 43.bxa3 as 43...♕e5+ 44.♕c3 ♖xc5 wins the knight and instead 44.♔b1 ♗f5 wins the queen.

9.♗c4 ♗d7 10.0-0-0 ♖b8

43...axb2+ 44.♔xb2 ♕d5

Now White is completely exposed.

45.♖c2 a4 46.♔a1 a3 47.♕e3 ♗f7 48.♕c3 g5 49.♕e3 ♖e8 50.♕c3 ♖e2 51.♘b3 ♖xc2 52.♕xc2 ♕e5+ 53.♔b1 ♔g7 54.♕d2 ♗xb3 0-1

Chapter 10

//

Odds and Ends

What follows are rarely played ideas for Black. "Rare" should not be interpreted as "unsound" – in fact, for the amateur player these are excellent weapons to mix into your rotation as your opponents are unlikely to be prepared for them. We will present three unique ideas, with two games for each one. All of the ideas involve queen moves – ...♛d8-b6, ...♛d8-b8, and ...♛d8-c7. Each move makes its own contribution to expanding your stock of ideas. Let's get to it.

1) 8.f3 ♛b6

Game 47

Hermansson, Emil (2423) – Yakovich, Yuri (2586) [B75]
Stockholm 2002

1.e4 c5 2.♘f3 ♘c6 3.♘c3 g6 4.d4 cxd4 5.♘xd4 ♝g7 6.♝e3 ♘f6 7.♝c4 d6 8.f3 ♛b6

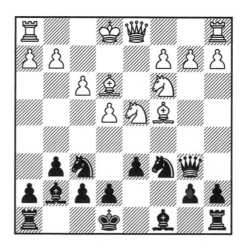

Yes, Black has indeed played 8...♛b6. No, it's not a mistake.

This move was first tried in the 1960s and it still makes an occasional appearance in games today. I experimented with in tournaments many years ago, with mixed results. The positions reached and resulting games were always fun. It's a rare treat in chess to play a move so early (8...♛b6) that utterly confounds your opponent. Often, he or she will sit and search for an outright refutation. Sometimes, after a minute or so, you can see the change come over their face as they fill up with hubris and slide the knight to f5, believing they've done great damage. Of course I would calmly reply with ...♛xb2, as it's the only move to be played.

9.♞f5 ♛xb2

Black must plunge in and mix it up. Black's edge is the element of surprise and the advantage of preparation, having worked out many of the lines at home; whereas White is very likely never to have seen the line before and must figure everything out in real time.

10.♞xg7+ ♚f8 11.♞d5 ♞xd5

These moves are also forced – neither White nor Black has any options here.

12.♝xd5 ♚xg7

White did have an option here, though not a good one. The game Rajković–Arnaudov, Ybbs 1968, went 12.♛xd5?. I strongly believe that this mistake is an example of seeing ahead to a critical position and making the wrong assessment. 12...♛xa1+ 13.♚e2 ♛xg7 14.♝h6. The immediate threat of mate created by the pin is one of the key positions White evaluated incorrectly. Black calmly plays 14...♝e6 and White has no idea that he is completely lost here: 15.♝xg7+ ♚xg7 16.♛d3 ♞e5 17.♛d4 ♝xc4+ 18.♚e1 g5 19.h4 h6 20.g3 f6 21.♚f2 ♜ac8 22.hxg5 hxg5 23.♜xh8 ♜xh8 24.♛xa7 ♜h2+ and White resigned. A crushing win and an example of how dangerous things can get if White is not careful.

13.♜b1 ♛c3+ 14.♚f2 f6

White has done just fine up to this point. He's stayed on track and made no mistakes.

15.g4

This move is a bit loose for my taste; the king still needs clothes as winter isn't over yet.

15...♘e5 16.h4 h5 17.gxh5 ♖xh5

Black has a slight edge thanks to his centralized and better-deployed pieces.

18.♗xb7 ♗xb7 19.♖xb7 ♔f8 20.f4

White could grab the pawn with 20.♖xa7, but this is not without risk. Black will not exchange rooks and will find a better square for his rook than a8.

20...♕c6 21.♖xa7

White can now capture the pawn, as the black rook must recapture in order to save the knight attacked by 20.f4.

21...♖xa7 22.♗xa7 ♘d7 23.♕f3 ♕xc2+

White gives up the c-pawn in order to hold the center. Far riskier is 23.♕d3 f5 24.♖h3 fxe4 25.♕c3 ♕a6 26.♕c7 ♘f6 27.♕b8+ ♔f7 28.♕b3+ d5 29.♗d4 ♖f5 30.♗xf6 ♕xf6 31.♔g2 ♕d6, when Black has a decisive edge.

24.♔g3 ♘c5 25.♖e1 ♕xa2 26.♗xc5 ♖xc5

In this type of position, the knight is stronger than the bishop, so White is happy to trade it off.

27.e5? dxe5

White's position is already difficult: he can't afford to blunder away a pawn.

28.fxe5 ♕a5!

Threatening the rook and overwhelming the pawn – how did White miss this?

29.♖e3 ♖xe5 30.♖a3 ♕e1+ 31.♔h3 ♖e4 0-1

There is no defense, as 32.♕g3 ♕h1+ 33.♕h2 ♖xh4 wins the queen. All other options are equally doomed.

Game 48

Zierk, Steven C. (2385) – Lee, Michael (2399) [B75]
ICC USA Team Tournament 2010

1.e4 c5 2.♘f3 ♘c6 3.♗c4 g6 4.d4 cxd4 5.♘xd4 ♗g7 6.♗e3 ♘f6 7.♘c3 d6 8.f3 ♕b6 9.♗b5

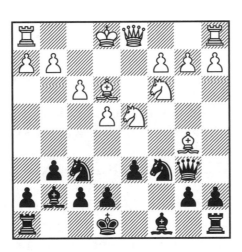

In the previous game, we witnessed a tactical battle with 9.♘f5 ♕xb2. Here, 9.♗b5 pins the knight and shields the b2 square, so ♘d4-f5 is still in the wind.

9...0-0 10.♘f5 ♕a5

Not only does Black not fear 10.♘f5, he dares White to play it by calmly castling and White takes up the challenge. A quick look at the position and you'd think Black must be in trouble, but that's just not the case – it's merely an exchange of some pieces.

11.♘xg7 ♚xg7 12.h4

Better for White is 12.♕d2 since it protects the c3-knight and threatens ♗e3-h6+ winning an exchange. Play might continue 12.♕d2 ♖d8 13.♗h6+ ♚g8 14.0-0 d5 15.♗xc6 bxc6 16.♖fd1 ♕b6+ 17.♗e3 ♕c7 18.♘a4, and the game is about equal here.

12...a6 13.♗xc6 bxc6 14.h5 ♚g8

If there is a lesson to be learned from this game, it is "calmness under fire." When you play the Dragon, you must conquer your fear. At times, you'll be on a razor's edge between winning and losing, so any self-doubt will hamper your ability to steer out of trouble and into the victory zone. This game is an excellent example of that ability in action.

15.♕d2 ♖b8

Black plays for the win with great courage. On 15...♘xh5 16.♗d4 e5 17.♖xh5 gxh5 18.♕g5+ ♚h8 19.♕f6+ ♚g8, White can draw with perpetual check, while playing on is risky: 20.♗e3 ♕d8 21.♕h6 ♕h4+ 22.♗f2 ♕e7 23.♕xh5 f6 and Black stands clearly better here.

16.0-0-0 ♗e6 17.♗d4 ♗xa2 18.♗xf6 exf6

A knight is a great defender of the king. Black was very brave to allow the knight to be chopped off the f6 square. Imagine this position in your mind, or set it up on a chessboard if you have trouble visualizing it. Take an empty board and place the black king on its home square (e8). Drop a white queen on e6, giving check to the king, now add a black knight on e7. The knight blocks the check and protects four other squares so that the queen can't give check.

19.♕xd6 ♗e6 20.hxg6 ♕a1+ 21.♚d2 ♕xb2 22.♕h2?

White doubles on the h-file, mistakenly believing that it's an unstoppable force. In fact, he blunders the game away. Correct is 22.gxh7+ ♔h8 23.♘a4 ♖fd8 24.♘xb2 ♖xd6+ 25.♘d3 a5, and White is better. If Black tries to tempo off the knight in this line, the game ends quickly with 22.gxh7+ ♔h8 23.♘a4 ♕a2 24.♕e7 ♔g7 25.♖h6!+−. If Black tries to keep the queens on, he simply runs out of ideas after 22.gxh7+ ♔h8 23.♘a4 ♕e5 24.♔e3 ♕g5+ 25.♔f2, when White is clearly on top.

22...♖fd8+

Having been given a second chance, Black walks over hot coals with no fear.

23.♘d5

Lobbing the knight onto d5 is actually a very good move in a losing position − it allows White counterchances and, if Black stumbles, he can turn the tables. Trying to run leads to checkmate or to massive loss of material followed by mate: 23.♔e2 ♕xc2+ 24.♔e1 ♕xc3+ 25.♔f2 ♕c5+ 26.♔g3 ♕g5+ 27.♔f2 ♖b2+ with mate to follow.

23...cxd5 24.♕xh7+

Another line of attack is to shred the kingside, but amazingly Black holds on for the win: 24.gxf7+ ♗xf7 25.♕xh7+ ♔f8 26.e5 fxe5 27.♕h6+ ♔e7 28.♕h4+ ♔d7 29.♕f6 ♕b4+ 30.♔e2 ♕c4+ 31.♔e1 d4−+.

24...♔f8 25.e5 ♕d4+ 26.♔e2 ♕xe5+ 27.♔f2 ♕f5

Black neutralizes every trick in White's playbook.

28.♖he1

No better is 28.g7+ ♔e7 29.g4 ♕xh7 30.♖xh7 ♖dc8 31.♖d2 f5 32.g5 a5 33.♔g3 a4 34.♖d4 ♖a8 − a piece down, it's hard to create enough complications to justify his position.

28...♕xc2+ 29.♖e2 ♕xd1 30.♖xe6 ♕c2+

Black is well aware that this is not checkers with mandatory re-captures, so he ignores the e6-rook as removing it allows mate at f7.

31.♖e2 ♕xg6 32.♕h8+ ♕g8 33.♕xf6 ♕g7 34.♕e7+ ♔g8 35.♖e5 ♖e8 0-1

One can only play on for so long a rook down. Lights out, game over.

2) 9.♗c4 ♗d7 10.0-0-0 ♕b8

Game 49

Liberzon, Vladimir (2540) – Parma, Bruno (2515) [B78]
Match, Athens 1976

1.e4 c5 2.♘f3 d6 3.d4 cxd4 4.♘xd4 ♘f6 5.♘c3 g6 6.♗e3 ♗g7 7.f3 ♘c6 8.♗c4 0-0 9.♕d2 ♗d7 10.0-0-0 ♕b8

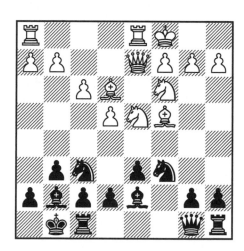

Credit for the novelty 10...♕b8 goes to GM Leonid Stein. Stein may be the strongest player never to become world champion. Un-fortunately, he died young and in his early career he was hidden in a Soviet system that contained a plethora of strong players and few opportunities. Stein's style is somewhat similar to that of Mikhail Tal, the main difference being that Tal played like a wizard, happy to run down a rabbit hole, while Stein was a scientist and less likely to enter into speculative attacks. One of the themes of this line is using the a8-rook right from where it sits.

11.h4 ♖c8

White signals that he intends to follow a standard Dragon kingside attack, and Black sets up the "magic formation." I have never played White's side of this position, but it must be a very imposing-looking setup to face with Black's major pieces all lined up in a row.

12.♗b3 a5

This is Black's best move and it offers fairly good chances. The next-best option here is 12...♘a5 and it is worthy of a try. The moves 12...b5 and 12...♘e5 have been tried, but they don't do terribly well and are better avoided altogether.

13.a3

This is too timid. White should play 13.a4, stopping 13...b5. This minor inaccuracy yields Black a tiny advantage.

13...b5 14.♘d5 ♘xd5

A very common theme is for White to play ♘c3-d5 with the idea of removing the f6-knight, as it's an excellent defender of the king.

15.♗xd5 b4

The pin (♗d5, ♘c6) is of minor importance because being up an exchange in a sharp Dragon line means nothing. It's all about active play and coordinating your minor pieces to conduct a successful attack.

16.a4 ♘xd4 17.♗xd4 e5 18.♗e3 ♗xa4

Yes, White can win the exchange; however, Black has his own shot on c2. Either White must play two rooks versus a queen or he must defend a difficult position that may not be defensible: 19.b3 ♗c6 20.♗c4 a4 21.h5 axb3 22.cxb3 ♗b5 23.♔b2 ♗xc4 24.bxc4 b3, and it's looking hard for White to hold.

19.♗xa8 ♖xc2+

White makes the right choice, providing him the greatest chance of turning the game around. I should point out that, all other things being equal, two rooks are very strong against a queen. The problem here is that all other things are not equal.

20.♕xc2 ♗xc2 21.♔xc2 ♕xa8 22.♖xd6 h5 23.♖hd1 ♕c8+ 24.♔b1 ♕c4 25.♖d8+ ♔h7

Black's queen is very active and his queenside pawn majority presents serious problems for the white king. Between moves 19 and 25, there was no way for White to improve the outcome, so the correct assessment may be that he was lost all along. If White mounts a blockade, the kingside pawns drop: 26.♖1d3 b3 27.♖8d7 ♕c2+ 28.♔a1 ♕xg2.

26.♖c1 ♕e2 27.♗b6 ♕xg2

Black's win of a pawn is just an insurance policy for the damage that he can still inflict upon the queenside.

28.♖d3 ♕e2 29.♖cd1 b3 30.♔a1 ♕c2 31.♖d5 ♕c6 32.♗c5 ♕a4+ 33.♗a3 ♗f8 0-1

Everything collapses. Resignation is the best move on the board here.

Game 50

Balaskas, Panayotis – Kaloskambis, Mihail [B78]
Greek Chp 1976

1.e4 c5 2.♘f3 d6 3.d4 cxd4 4.♘xd4 ♘f6 5.♘c3 g6 6.♗e3 ♗g7 7.f3 ♘c6 8.♕d2 0-0 9.♗c4 ♗d7 10.0-0-0 ♕b8 11.h4 ♖c8 12.♗b3 a5 13.a4

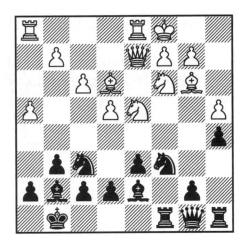

In this game, White plays the recommended 13.a4. Let's see how Black can create some magic against an opponent who knows a bit of theory.

13...♘xd4 14.♗xd4 b5 15.axb5

Exchanging pawns plays into Black's plans. White should try to counter in the center with ideas like 15.♘d5 e5 16.♗xe5 dxe5 17.♘xf6+ ♗xf6 18.♕xd7 ♖a7 19.♕d6 bxa4 20.♕xb8 ♖xb8, when he stands better.

15...♗xb5 16.♗xf6 ♗xf6 17.♘d5 a4 18.♘xf6+ exf6

White has managed to release the center pressure and busted up Black's pawns. However, this has come at the cost of accelerating Black's attack. Black now has the advantage.

19.♗a2

Too passive. White should forgo Black's weak d-pawn; it can be won later on. Instead, he needs to anchor the bishop with 19.♗d5, where it can assist in defending the queenside without getting in the way.

19...a3 20.b3

After 19...a3, White had to play 20.b3 but this does highlight how passive 19.♗a2 was.

20...♖a6 21.♕d4 ♖ac6 22.♖d2 ♖c3 23.♔b1 ♕c7 24.♖c1

A better defensive plan is to trade off some major pieces with 24.♕xd6 ♖xc2 25.♕xc7 ♖2xc7 26.b4 ♖c3 27.♗d5, when White is still behind but his position is defendable.

24...♗d3 25.♕f2?

Best defense is 25.♔a1 ♗xc2 26.b4 ♔g7 27.♗d5 ♕e7 28.g4 ♕e5 29.♕xe5 dxe5. Black stands better, but there is still hope for White.

25...♖xb3+ 26.♗xb3 ♕c3 27.cxd3 ♕xb3+ 28.♖b2 a2+ 0-1

There was no defense; the following bizarre idea would offer a glimmer of hope if the bishop did not drop: 27.♕d4? ♕xd4 28.cxd3 ♖xc1+ 29.♔xc1 ♕a1+ 30.♔c2 ♕b2+ and now the bishop and the game are lost.

3) 9.♗c4 ♗d7 10.0-0-0 ♕c7

Game 51
___
Moldovan, Daniel (2420) – Vesselovsky, Serguei (2435) [B78]
Hollabrunn 1998

1.e4 c5 2.♘f3 d6 3.d4 cxd4 4.♘xd4 ♘f6 5.♘c3 g6 6.♗e3 ♗g7 7.f3 ♘c6 8.♕d2 0-0 9.♗c4 ♗d7 10.0-0-0 ♕c7

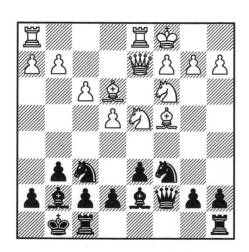

This is a seldom-played line, but it has merit and is worth trying at least for shock value. Black places the queen on c7 with an indirect threat on the c4-bishop. Most often, White moves the bishop right away to deal with the threat as quickly as possible. If White instead plays either knight to b5, we can retreat the queen to b8 or c8 and kick the misplaced knight with ...a7-a6, for example 11.♘cb5 ♕c8 12.♗e2 a6 13.♘c3 b5 and White has only altered his position by moving his bishop to e2, whereas Black has slipped in two very useful pawn moves.

11.♗b3 ♖fc8 12.h4 ♘a5

Black has doubled on the c-file and cleared the way for ...b7-b5. This is a very reasonable position for Black to launch an attack from.

13.h5 ♘xb3+ 14.cxb3 b5

Thanks to the pin, ...b7-b5 comes for free. After 14.axb3 ♘xh5 15.g4 ♘f6 16.♔b1 ♕a5 17.♗h6 ♗xh6 18.♕xh6 ♖xc3 19.bxc3 ♕xc3, White is slightly better. Or 14.axb3 ♕a5 15.♔b1 e5 16.♘de2 ♖c6 17.♘d5 ♕xd2 18.♘xf6+ ♗xf6 19.♖xd2 and it's close to equal.

15.♔b1 b4 16.♘d5 ♘xd5 17.exd5 ♕a5

The opening of the c-file gives Black a small edge.

18.hxg6 fxg6 19.♗h6 ♗f6

Of course, without the black knight to defend, the bishop trade must be avoided.

20.♗g5?

White must play 20.♘e6 to obstruct Black's powerful light-squared bishop.

20...♗xd4 21.♕xd4 ♗f5+ 22.♔a1 ♖c5

Black threatens ...♕xa2+ and ...♖a5 with mate. Now it's easy to see why 20.♘e6 was the only move.

23.♖d3

This move stops mate, but that's about all that can be said for it.

23...e5 24.dxe6 ♗xd3 25.♕xd3 ♖xg5

Suddenly, White is a full rook down with a weak passed pawn to show for it.

26.♕xd6 ♕d8 27.♕xb4 ♕c7 0-1

Game 52

Guzikov, Danil – Zaitsev, Vadim (2356) [B78]
Novokuznetsk 2011

1.e4 c5 2.♘f3 d6 3.d4 cxd4 4.♘xd4 ♘f6 5.♘c3 g6 6.f3 ♗g7 7.♗c4 ♘c6 8.♗e3 0-0 9.♕d2 ♗d7 10.0-0-0 ♕c7 11.♗b3 ♖fc8 12.h4 ♘e5

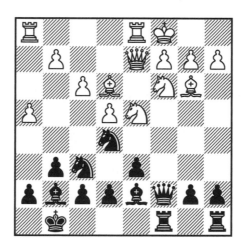

In Game 51, the knight jumped to a5, while here the knight lands on e5. Both moves control c4; the difference is that, whereas the centralized knight exerts pressure on f3, the knight on the wing can eliminate White's bishop with ...♘xb3.

13.♗h6 ♗h8

I have great affection for this move, which retains the Dragon bishop. It's a nice option to have at your disposal, so getting the rook off f8 early is always a good idea if you want to be able to play ...♗h8.

14.h5 ♘c4 15.♗xc4 ♕xc4 16.hxg6 fxg6

Recapturing the pawn is not an either-or situation – 16...fxg6 is necessary, as Black can find himself in trouble after 16...hxg6 17.♘f5 ♗xf5 (the knight cannot be taken by the pawn, as mate ensues after 18.♕g5+) 18.exf5 ♖c5 19.fxg6 fxg6 20.♗e3.

17.♔b1 b5 18.♘b3 ♗e6

Black's pieces are all very well coordinated and aiming at White's queenside.

19.♘d5 ♘xd5

Also possible is 19...♗xd5 20.exd5 a5 21.♖he1 ♖c7 22.c3 a4 23.♕e3 (threatening mate) 23...e5 (only move) 24.♘d2 ♕c5 25.♕xc5 ♖xc5, and Black is fine. The risk-reward assessment here is that 19...♗xd5 offers more defensive chances for Black and fewer attacking chances, while 19...♘xd5 offers greater attacking chances but leaves Black open to counterattacks.

20.exd5 ♗f5 21.♖c1 a5

From f5, the bishop puts extreme pressure on White and he must guard c1 with his rook – which, however, weakens the d4 square. The c1-rook also denies the b3-knight an escape square.

22.g4 ♗d7 23.♗g5 a4

There is no easy defense after 22...a4. Black is winning after 24.♘a5 ♖xa5 25.♕xa5 ♕d4 26.c3 ♕xd5 27.♗xe7 ♗e6 28.c4 ♕d3+ 29.♖c2 ♗xc4 30.♖hc1 ♖e8 31.♗g5 ♕xf3.

24.♕h2 h5

White swings over to the kingside to threaten Black and create an escape square for his knight. The downside is that the queen is no longer helping to protect the king.

25.♘d2 ♕d4 26.c3 ♕d3+ 27.♖c2 b4

White is crushed: there is nothing left to do but to go through the motions and hope that Black blunders.

28.gxh5 ♗f5 29.♘e4 b3 30.♔a1 ♕xc2 31.♕h4 a3 0-1

Mate is unstoppable (32.♖b1 axb2+ 33.♖xb2 ♖xa2+ 34.♖xa2 ♕xa2#).

Book 2: Quizzes

Introduction

I struggled with the proper title for this section and finally settled on "Quizzes." I call them quizzes with great reservations, though. *There are positions with one correct answer that justify the idea of a "quiz" or a "test." Not all of the positions here have one single answer, others do not lead to a clearly won position, and still others present new ideas with material that was not covered in the first part of this book.* Not being totally satisfied with the term "quiz," I returned to my original idea for this book: the goal of enlightenment, patterns, *ZOOM 001*, and osmosis. Tossing these words into the air, they landed on my keyboard saying, "The *ZOOM 001* quiz of patterns and osmosis by enlightenment." I think we'd all admit that's way over the top. So with no better title, I'm leaving it as "quizzes," but I want you to view this as *your* section, not mine. Approach it as your personal bank account of ideas. I am merely assisting you in opening the account. It is your idea bank, a place where you can withdraw new ideas and refresh and revisit ones you already own. If this process encourages you to begin that journey of expanding your chess senses, then I will consider this work a huge success.

The format for the quiz section is as follows: the quiz number (or if you prefer, the Idea Bank Number) followed by a diagram.

In the solutions section, you will see either:

Game X, Player–Player

or:

Player – Player
Tournament/City YEAR
(game does not appear in book).

The Quizzes

Quiz 1

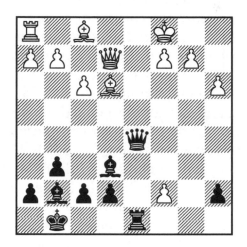

Black to move

Quiz 2

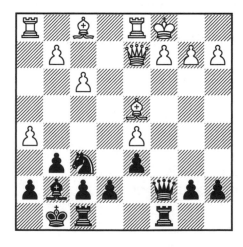

Black to move

Quiz 3

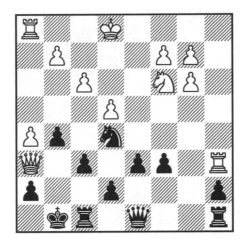

Black to move

Quiz 4

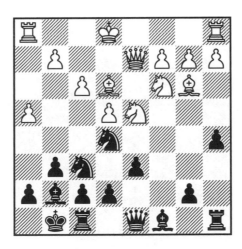

Black to move

Quiz 5

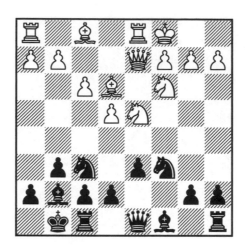

Black to move

Quiz 6

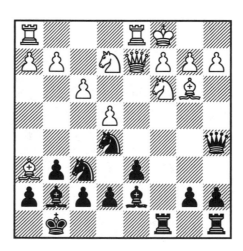

Black to move

Quiz 7

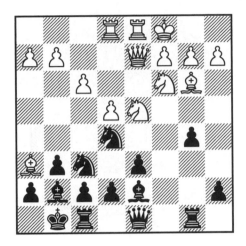

Black to move

Quiz 8

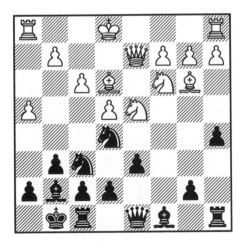

Black to move

Quiz 9

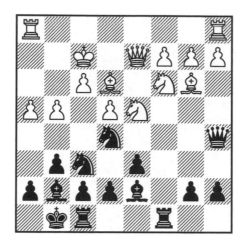

Black to move

Quiz 10

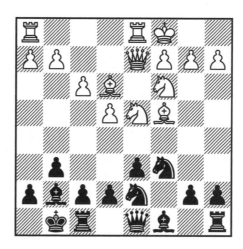

Black to move

Quiz 11

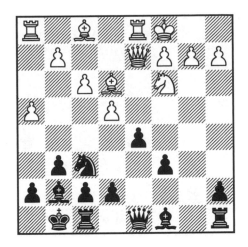

Black to move

Quiz 12

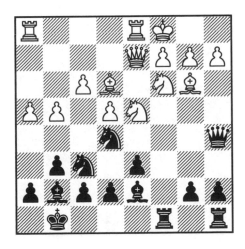

Black to move

Quiz 13

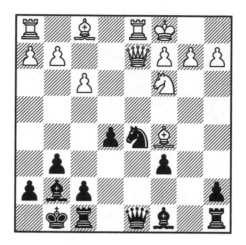

Black to move

Quiz 14

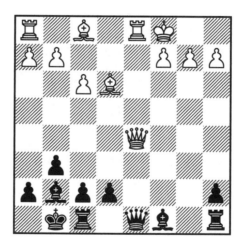

Black to move

Quiz 15

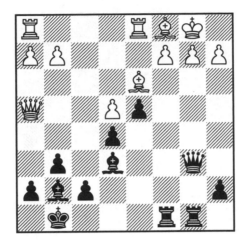

Black to move

Quiz 16

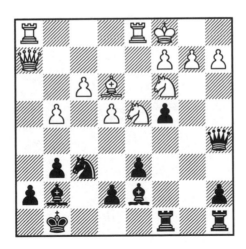

Black to move

Quiz 17

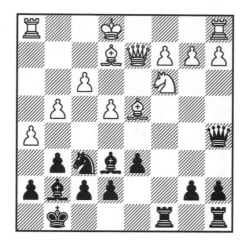

Black to move

Quiz 18

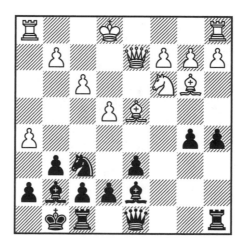

Black to move

Quiz 19

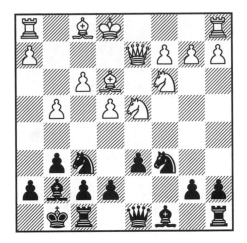

Black to move

Quiz 20

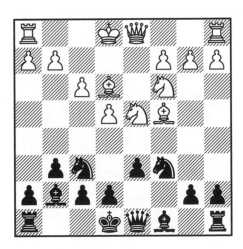

Black to move

Quiz 21

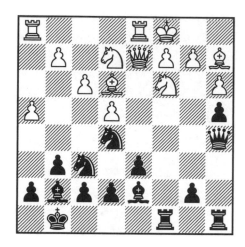

Black to move

Quiz 22

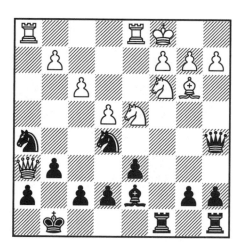

Black to move

Quiz 23

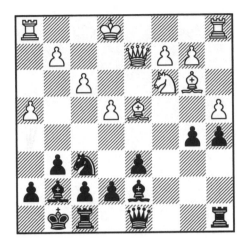

Black to move

Quiz 24

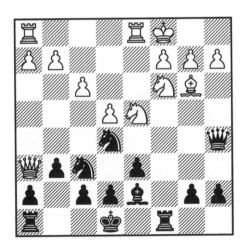

Black to move

Quiz 25

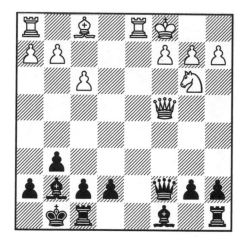

Black to move

Quiz 26

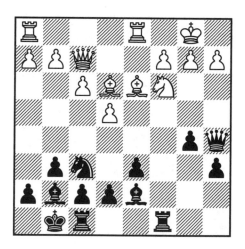

Black to move

Quiz 27

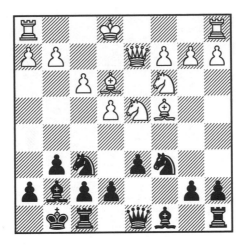

Black to move

Quiz 28

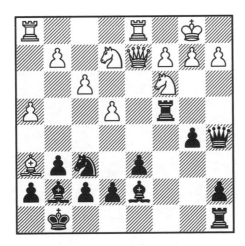

Black to move

Quiz 29

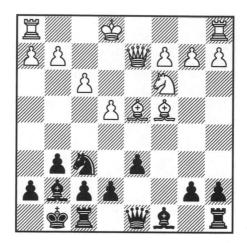

Black to move

Quiz 30

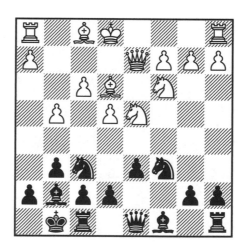

Black to move

Quiz 31

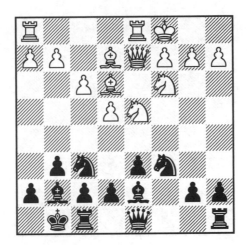

Black to move

Quiz 32

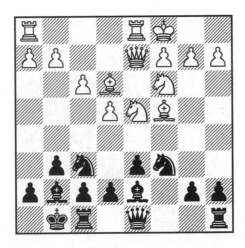

Black to move

Quiz 33

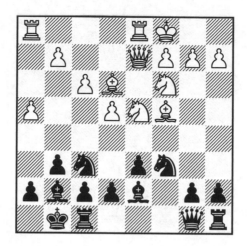

Black to move

Quiz 34

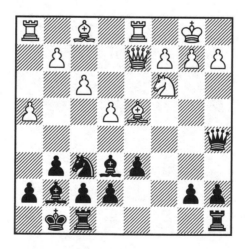

Black to move

Quiz 35

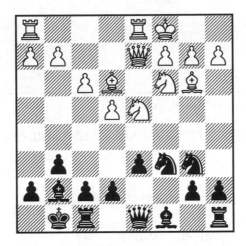

Black to move

Quiz 36

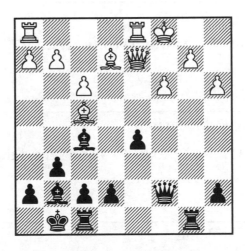

Black to move

Solutions to the Quizzes

Quiz 1

Game 26, Voitsikh–Rusinkevich

Black plays **18...♗xb2** 19.♔xb2 ♕a2+ and mate next move is unstoppable.

Quiz 2

Game 8, Pustelny-Conrad–Sehner

14...♗h6 draws White's queen away from defending the mate at c2.

Quiz 3

Game 3, Marinova–Velcheva

White found her queen trapped after **17...♘f7**.

Quiz 4

Game 35, Efimov–Zilberstein

Black played **11...a4** 12.♗xa4 ♘c4 and seized the advantage.

Quiz 5

Game 27, Byvshev–Beilin

Actually, it could be any of several games: Black took his shot to open up the center with **9...d5**.

Quiz 6

Game 39, Seck–Velásquez

Black played **13...♞c4**, and after the exchange he went on to double rooks on the semi-open c-file.

Quiz 7

Game 43, Könnyű–Sedlak

Black played **13...♝xh6**, and after 14.♛xh6 a5, White replied 15.a4 and quickly fell apart.

Quiz 8

Game 33, Hloušek –Kølbæk

Black played **11...a4** 12.♞xa4 ♜xa4!! 13.♝xa4 ♞c4 14.♛c3 ♞xe3 15.♔f2 ♞eg4+ and went on to crush White.

Quiz 9

Gerbec, Theodor – Colle, Edgar [B77]
Bad Oeynhausen 1922
(game does not appear in book)

1.e4 c5 2.♞f3 ♞c6 3.d4 cxd4 4.♞xd4 ♞f6 5.♞c3 d6 6.♝c4 ♝d7 7.f3 g6 8.♝e3 ♝g7 9.♛d2 0-0 10.g4 ♜c8 11.♝b3 ♛a5 12.h4 ♞e5 13.♔f2 *(quiz position)*.

13...♞exg4+ 14.fxg4 ♜xc3 (White can't recapture due to ...♞xe4+ forking king and queen) 15.♝d5 ♞xg4+ 0-1.

Quiz 10

Gimmelman – Gorodezky, A. [B77]
USSR 1962
(game does not appear in book)

1.e4 c5 2.♞f3 d6 3.d4 cxd4 4.♞xd4 ♞f6 5.♞c3 g6 6.♝e3 ♝g7 7.f3 0-0 8.♝c4 ♞c6 9.♛d2 ♞d7 10.0-0-0 *(quiz position)*.

Black invoked the "traveling knights" idea and won quickly after trapping the white queen: **10...♘b6** 11.♗b3 ♘a5 12.♗h6 ♘bc4 13.♕g5 e5 14.♘de2 ♗f6 15.♕g3 ♗h4 0-1.

Quiz 11

Game 29, Sorri–Arnaudov

Black goes for a solid center: **11...♗e6** 12.e5 ♘d7 13.♗h6 ♗xe5 14.♗xf8 ♕xf8.

Quiz 12

Game 41, Mnatsakanian–Veresov

Black played without fear and went on to win after **13...♖c4!** 14.♗xc4 ♘xc4 15.♕d3 b5 16.♘b3 ♕a6 17.♗d4 e5 18.♗f2 b4.

Quiz 13

Game 30, Ljubojević–Svensson

White has just played 13.♗c5, attacking the f8-rook. Black forged ahead with development and played **13...♗e6**, with the game continuing 14.♗c4 ♘xc3 15.♗xe6 ♘xd1 16.♗d7 ♘xb2 17.♔xb2 ♖b8+ 18.♔c1 ♖b7 0-1.

Quiz 14

Chicote Franco, Guillermo – Martín González, Ángel [B76]
Ponferrada Open, Spain 1992
(game does not appear in book)

1.e4 c5 2.♘f3 d6 3.d4 cxd4 4.♘xd4 ♘f6 5.♘c3 g6 6.f3 ♗g7 7.♗e3 ♘c6 8.♕d2 0-0 9.0-0-0 d5 10.exd5 ♘xd5 11.♘xc6 bxc6 12.♘xd5 cxd5 13.♕xd5 *(quiz position)*.

Black played **13...♕c7**, leaving the rook hanging, and won after 14.♕xa8 ♗f5 15.♕xf8+ ♔xf8 16.♗d3 ♕e5 17.♔d2 ♗xd3 18.♔xd3 ♕xb2 19.♔e2 ♕xc2+ 20.♖d2 ♕c4+ 21.♔f2 ♗c3 22.♗h6+ ♔e8 23.♖e2 0-1.

Quiz 15

Sánchez Piquero, Javier – González Valdés, José Luis [B76]
Asturias Team Chp, Spain 1987
(game does not appear in book)

1.e4 c5 2.♘f3 d6 3.d4 cxd4 4.♘xd4 ♘f6 5.♘c3 g6 6.♗e3 ♗g7 7.f3 0-0 8.♕d2 ♘c6 9.0-0-0 d5 10.♕f2 e5 11.♘xc6 bxc6 12.exd5 cxd5 13.♗g5 d4 14.♕h4 ♕b6 15.♘e4 ♘xe4 16.fxe4 ♗e6 17.♔b1 ♖fc8 18.♗d3 ♖ab8 19.♗c1 *(quiz position)*.

Black wins the game with a super rook: **19...♖c3!** 20.♖d2 ♗xa2+ 21.♔xa2 ♖a3+!! 22.♔b1 ♕a5 0-1.

Quiz 16

Game 38, Äijälä–Ljubojević

Black ignores the pressure on the semi-open h-file and brings his queen rook into the game: **17...♖ab8** 18.♘d5 c3 19.♘xf6+ exf6 20.♕xh7+ ♔f7 21.♘f5 gxf5 22.♖xd6 cxb2+ 23.♔b1 ♕a4 24.♖d2 ♖h8 0-1.

Quiz 17

Game 15, Shimanov–Kabanov

Black controls the c4 square: **13...♗c4** 14.hxg6 hxg6 15.g5 ♘h5.

Quiz 18

Petr, Martin (2451) – Chuprov, Dmitry (2577) [B77]
Pardubice Open, Czech Republic 2008
(game does not appear in book)

1.e4 c5 2.♘f3 ♘c6 3.♘c3 g6 4.d4 cxd4 5.♘xd4 ♗g7 6.♗e3 ♘f6 7.♗c4 0-0 8.♗b3 d6 9.f3 ♗d7 10.♕d2 ♘xd4 11.♗xd4 b5 12.h4 a5 13.h5 *(quiz position)*.

13...a4 appears to win a piece, but 14.♗xf6 exf6 15.♗d5 and the bishop escapes to freedom. Chess is a hard game! However, after

15...b4 16.♘e2 f5! Black does get a nice attack going. The game ended 17.hxg6 hxg6 18.♗xa8 ♕xa8 19.♕xb4 fxe4 20.0-0 ♕a7+ 21.♖f2 exf3 22.gxf3 ♖b8 23.♕xd6 a3 24.♖b1 axb2 25.♔g2 ♗e6 0-1.

Quiz 19

Noskov, Anatolij – Losev, Dmitry [B76]
Russian Winter Open, Moscow 1991
(game does not appear in book)

1.e4 c5 2.♘f3 d6 3.d4 cxd4 4.♘xd4 ♘f6 5.♘c3 g6 6.♗e3 ♗g7 7.f3 ♘c6 8.♕d2 0-0 9.g4 *(quiz position)*.

Black created wonderful complications after **9...♗xg4** 10.♘xc6 bxc6 11.fxg4 ♘xg4 12.♗d4 e5 13.♗f2 ♗h6. You should look for ways to exploit this pattern of sacrificing a piece for two pawns at g4 where the anchored knight will support ...♗g7-h6.

14.♕e2 f5 15.♗g3 ♖b8 16.♘d1 ♖xb2 17.♗h3 ♕a5+ 18.♔f1 ♘e3+ 19.♘xe3 ♗xe3 20.♕c4+ d5 21.♕d3 fxe4+ 0-1.

Quiz 20

Rajković, Dušan – Arnaudov, Petar
World Team U26 Chp, Ybbs 1968
(game does not appear in book)

1.e4 c5 2.♘c3 ♘c6 3.♘f3 g6 4.d4 cxd4 5.♘xd4 ♗g7 6.♗e3 ♘f6 7.♗c4 d6 8.f3 *(quiz position)*.

Black played the unorthodox **8...♕b6**, a rarely played move that we examined in Games 47 and 48. Because this move is so seldom tried, there is value in uncorking this idea for shock effect. It is very unlikely your opponents will have faced this before and you can end up with some very exciting and quick games. Chess is a very rich game and you should feel free to investigate new ideas early and often.

Black went on give up his queen and won a crazy game: 9.♘f5 ♕xb2 10.♘xg7+ ♔f8 11.♘d5 ♘xd5 12.♕xd5 ♕xa1+ 13.♔e2 ♕xg7 14.♗h6 ♗e6 15.♗xg7+ ♔xg7 16.♕d3 ♘e5 17.♕d4 ♗xc4+ 18.♔e1 g5

19.h4 h6 20.g3 f6 21.♔f2 ♖ac8 22.hxg5 hxg5 23.♖xh8 ♖xh8 24.♕xa7 ♖h2+ 0-1.

Quiz 21

Game 34, Frilling–Watson

Black played **15...♗e6**, attacking White's a2-bishop. The game quickly erupts into massive fireworks, so review this game again!

Quiz 22

Outerelo Ucha, Manuel – Hoffman, Alejandro [B79]
Aceimar Open, Mondariz (Spain) 2003
(game does not appear in book)

1.e4 c5 2.♘f3 d6 3.d4 cxd4 4.♘xd4 ♘f6 5.♘c3 g6 6.♗e3 ♗g7 7.f3 ♘c6 8.♕d2 ♗d7 9.♗c4 0-0 10.0-0-0 ♕a5 11.h4 ♘e5 12.♗b3 ♖fc8 13.h5 ♘xh5 14.♗h6 ♗xh6 15.♕xh6 *(quiz position)*.

Black played **15...♖xc3**, removing the knight from the board so that White would no longer have ♘d5 as an answer to 16...♘f6, slowing down White's kingside attack.

The game proceeded 16.bxc3 ♘f6 17.♘e2 ♖c8 18.♔b1 ♘c4 19.♖d5 ♕c7 20.♘f4 ♘a3+ 21.♔b2 ♕xc3+ 22.♔xa3 ♖c6 0-1.

Quiz 23

Baljon, Christofoor – da Silva, Fernando Pires [B77]
Groningen 1971
(game does not appear in book)

1.e4 c5 2.♘f3 ♘c6 3.d4 cxd4 4.♘xd4 g6 5.♘c3 ♗g7 6.♗e3 ♘f6 7.♗c4 0-0 8.♗b3 d6 9.f3 ♗d7 10.♕d2 ♘xd4 11.♗xd4 b5 12.h4 a5 13.a4 *(quiz position)*.

In reply to 13.a4, Black played **13...bxa4**. Black could have easily opted for 13...b5, kicking the knight. However, it is often better to pry open the b-file and create complications: (13...bxa4) 14.♘xa4 e5 15.♗c3 ♗e6 16.0-0-0 ♗xb3 17.cxb3 ♕b8 18.♕xd6 ♕xb3 19.♘c5 ♕c4 20.♘d3 a4 21.♘xe5 ♕a2 22.♘c6 a3 23.♘e7+ ♔h8 24.bxa3 ♖ab8 0-1

Quiz 24

Game 40, Ermakov–Hamburg

White has just castled long, and Black plays the thematic exchange sacrifice: **13...♖xc3** 14.bxc3 ♕xc3 15.♘e2 ♘d3+ 16.♖xd3 ♕a1+.

This position also contains another example of our ...♘d3+ trick to win back the exchange. I've seen countless speed games where players should play this and don't. That's an indication that the idea is not yet part of their chess DNA.

Quiz 25

Game 32, Hadjittofis–Whiteley

White has just played 15.♕c4, offering to exchange queens. Black plays **15...♕b6** 16.♗d3 ♕f6 17.c3 ♗e6, and we can explain Black's play because he wants to have his queen on the board for attacking purposes. It's also worth pointing out, as a general precept, not to make trades that leave your opponent more active.

Quiz 26

Bellón López, Juan Manuel – Adorján, András [B76]
Groningen 1969
(game does not appear in book)

1.e4 c5 2.♘f3 ♘c6 3.d4 cxd4 4.♘xd4 g6 5.♘c3 ♗g7 6.♗e3 ♘f6 7.♗c4 0-0 8.f3 d6 9.♕e2 ♗d7 10.0-0-0 ♘a5 11.♗d3 ♖c8 12.♔b1 a6 13.♘b3 b5 14.♘xa5 ♕xa5 15.♕f2 (quiz position).

White has just moved his queen further away from the defense of the king. Black jumps on the exchange sacrifice thus: **15...♖xc3** 16.bxc3 ♕xc3 17.♔c1 ♖c8 18.♗d4 ♕b4.

You should not be so cavalier as to sacrifice the exchange without analyzing the position. However, I would encourage you to find a strong reason *not* to play the sacrifice. Otherwise, just play it and smile.

19.♕g1 ♗e6 20.♖d2 ♗xa2 21.♔d1 e5 22.♗a1 ♗h6 23.♕e1 ♗c4 24.♗xc4 ♖xc4 25.♔e2 ♘xe4 0-1.

Quiz 27

Babovich – Szyszko-Bohusz, Andrzej [B77]
Poland 1975
(game does not appear in book)

1.e4 c5 2.♘f3 d6 3.d4 cxd4 4.♘xd4 ♘f6 5.♘c3 g6 6.♗c4 ♗g7 7.f3 0-0 8.♗e3 ♘c6 9.♕d2 *(quiz position)*.

White has just played 9.♕d2 and our answer is a bit of a trick question: **9...♕c7**. This idea was covered in Games 51 and 52 as 10...♕c7 – the move order is a bit different but the theme is the same. Do not be afraid to experiment – it worked out well in this game!

10.♗b3 ♗d7 11.g4 ♖fc8 12.h4 ♘e5 13.0-0-0 ♘c4 14.♗xc4 ♕xc4 15.h5 b5 16.hxg6 b4 17.gxf7+ ♔xf7 18.♘b1 ♕xa2 19.g5 ♘d5 20.exd5 ♗f5 21.♖h2 b3 22.♕b4 bxc2 23.♘xc2 ♖ab8 24.♖d4 ♖xb4 0-1.

Quiz 28

Rueetschi, Urs – Ernst, Thomas [B79]
Eeklo (Belgium) 1979
(game does not appear in book)

1.e4 c5 2.♘f3 d6 3.d4 cxd4 4.♘xd4 ♘f6 5.♘c3 g6 6.♗e3 ♗g7 7.f3 0-0 8.♕d2 ♘c6 9.♗c4 ♗d7 10.0-0-0 ♕a5 11.h4 ♘e5 12.♗b3 ♖fc8 13.♔b1 ♘c4 14.♗xc4 ♖xc4 15.♘de2 b5 16.♗h6 *(quiz position)*.

White has just played 16.♗h6 and Black replies **16...b4**.

If you thought the answer might be 16...♗xh6, then know that after the queen is drawn away to play ...♖xc3, it never works well when the knights are connected. We need to double the pawns in front of White's king for the exchange sacrifice to be effective. And if the knights are connected, we can't do a double rook sacrifice, as it leaves us too few pieces to do battle with.

The game continued with (16.♗h6 b4) 17.♘d5 ♘xd5 18.♗xg7 ♔xg7, and Black soon won with a big surprise: 19.exd5 ♖ac8 20.h5 ♖xc2 21.♕d4+ f6 22.hxg6 ♗f5 23.♔a1 b3 24.a3 ♕xa3+ 0-1.

Quiz 29

Game 22, Vertesi–Teufel

Black has just exchanged knights and White has recaptured with 10.♗xd4. Black plays **10...♗e6**, challenging the c4-bishop to exchange or retreat. Play continued using 11.♗b3 ♕a5 12.0-0-0 ♗xb3 13.cxb3 ♖fc8 with an equal position. However, it is important to know that Black has nothing to fear from the exchange 11.♗xe6 fxe6 12.0-0-0 ♕a5.

Quiz 30

Thorisson, S. – Kudrin, Sergey [B76]
Gausdal 1982
(game does not appear in book)

1.e4 c5 2.♘f3 d6 3.d4 cxd4 4.♘xd4 ♘f6 5.♘c3 g6 6.f3 ♗g7 7.♗e3 ♘c6 8.♕d2 0-0 9.g4 *(quiz position)*.

In this position, Black decided to take time with **9...e6** to build a solid center to secure his attack. The game continued 10.h4 d5 11.♘xc6 bxc6 12.0-0-0 ♕a5 13.exd5 ♖b8, when Black was at least equal. It is worth noting that after 9.g4, some hyper-aggressive players have played 9...♗xg4 10.fxg4 ♘xg4, with complications.

Thorisson–Kudrin concluded with 14.♗d4 exd5 15.♗xf6 ♗xf6 16.♕f4 ♗f5 17.gxf5 ♖xb2 18.♖d3 ♗xc3 19.fxg6 hxg6 20.h5 ♖fb8 21.♔d1 ♖e8 22.♖e3 ♖xe3 0-1.

Quiz 31

Walter – Kettner, Jürgen [B76]
Konstanz 1983
(game does not appear in book)

1.e4 c5 2.♘f3 d6 3.d4 cxd4 4.♘xd4 ♘f6 5.♘c3 g6 6.♗e2 ♗g7 7.♗e3 0-0 8.♕d2 ♘c6 9.0-0-0 ♗d7 10.f3 *(quiz position)*.

White has just played 10.f3. If you consider the idea 10...♘xd4 11.♗xd4 and 11...♕a5 or 11...♗e6, that's reasonable given the material we've covered. However, chess is a rich game with lots of choices, and here Black chooses **10...♕b8**. Black had a wide-open attack following 11.g4 ♖c8 12.h4 b5 13.♗xb5 ♘xd4, and won after 14.♗xd7 ♘xf3 15.♕e2 ♘xd7 16.♘a4 ♕b4 17.b3 ♘b6 18.♗xb6 axb6 19.♕xf3 ♖xa4 20.bxa4 ♗b2+ 0-1.

Quiz 32

Refskalevsky, Carlos – Mascarenhas, Alberto Pinheiro [B78]
Brazilian Chp, Brasília 1985
(game does not appear in book)

1.e4 c5 2.♘f3 d6 3.d4 cxd4 4.♘xd4 ♘f6 5.♘c3 g6 6.♗e3 ♗g7 7.f3 ♘c6 8.♕d2 0-0 9.♗c4 ♗d7 10.0-0-0 *(quiz position)*.

If you recognized that this position allows many options covered in this book, then good for you! However, like the previous game, Black played ...♕d8-b8 here too: **10...♕b8** 11.♗b3 ♖c8 12.h4 a5 13.♘xc6 ♗xc6 14.a3 b5 15.♘d5 ♗xd5 16.♗xd5 ♘xd5 17.exd5 b4 18.a4 b3 19.c3 ♕b4 20.♗d4 ♕xa4 21.♕e3 ♗xd4 0-1.

Quiz 33

Meyer, Jürgen – Jess, Arne [B78]
Schleswig-Holstein Chp, Glücksburg (Germany) 1988
(game does not appear in book)

1.e4 c5 2.♘f3 d6 3.d4 cxd4 4.♘xd4 ♘f6 5.♘c3 g6 6.♗e3 ♗g7 7.f3 ♘c6 8.♕d2 0-0 9.♗c4 ♗d7 10.0-0-0 ♕b8 11.h4 *(quiz position)*.

OK, so in this game you know he's played 10...♕b8. No more tricks! Now the question is, what did he do after 11.h4 ? The answer is that he attacked at once with **11...b5** 12.♘dxb5 ♖c8 13.♘a3 ♕b7 14.♗b3 a5 15.♗h6 ♗h8 16.♘ab1 ♘b4 17.a4 ♖ab8 18.♘b5 ♗xb5 19.axb5 ♕xb5 20.♘c3 ♘a2+ 21.♘xa2 ♕xb3 0-1.

Quiz 34

Game 9, Ziska–Jakobsen

White played 12.♔b1, and Black answers with **12...♖fc8** in order not to be caught off-guard with 13.♘d5. If you are not sure why this is a good idea, please review the game, as it's a frequent theme. 13...♕xd2 14.♖xd2 ♗xd5 15.♗xf6 ♗xa2+, and Black has the advantage.

Quiz 35

Game 1, MacDonald–Zube

Black has played our ...♘f6-d7 theme, followed by ...♘b6. Play continues with **11...♘a5** 12.♗h6 ♘bc4 13.♕g5 e5, when Black has the game locked down with his super knights.

Quiz 36

Unkelbach, R. – Christoffel, Ulrich [B76]
Trier (Germany) 1991
(game does not appear in book)

1.e4 c5 2.♘f3 d6 3.d4 cxd4 4.♘xd4 ♘f6 5.♘c3 g6 6.♗e3 ♗g7 7.f3 0-0 8.♕d2 ♘c6 9.♗e2 d5 10.exd5 ♘xd5 11.♘xc6 bxc6 12.♘xd5 cxd5 13.0-0-0 ♖b8 14.c3 ♕c7 15.a3 ♗f5 16.♗f4 *(quiz position)*.

Black brings home the point with **16...♖xb2** 17.♕xb2 ♕xf4+ 18.♕d2 ♕a4 0-1.

Closing Thoughts

My intent in writing this book is to share my experience, to teach a few humble lessons, and to learn through the journey and your feedback. Therefore, I strongly encourage you to join my mailing list and share your thoughts with me. (All you have to do is go to www.chessmastercoach.com and sign up.)

Sharing from my patzer years to my master years has enabled me to rediscover the wonderful journey I've been so fortunate to travel. If you would like to learn more about my early chess years and what kick-started me along the way, read my Amazon Kindle primer, *Chess Patzer to Master – How an Everyday Joe Does It*.

Succeeding at chess is just like succeeding at life: it requires tenacity and a belief in yourself. It requires you to challenge yourself and to question your preconceived perception of life, on and off the board. You must take risks and be willing to lose in order to grow. Setting goals, having a life plan, and working harder on yourself than you do on your job are all critical elements that may very well be the subject of a future book, so sign up for my list!